Build your own
WEBSITE

**Everything you need
to know, explained clearly
in plain English**

Davey Winder

Prentice
Hall

An imprint of **Pearson Education**
London · New York · Toronto · Sydney · Tokyo · Singapore
Madrid · Mexico City · Munich · Paris

PEARSON EDUCATION LIMITED

Head Office
Edinburgh Gate
Harlow CM20 2JE
Tel: +44 (0)1279 623623
Fax: +44 (0)1279 431059

London Office:
128 Long Acre
London WC2E 9AN
Tel: +44 (0)20 7447 2000
Fax: +44 (0)20 7240 5771
Website: *www.informit.uk.com*

This edition published in Great Britain in 2001
First published in Great Britain by VNU Business Publications in 2000

© VNU Business Publications 2001

ISBN 0-130-61232-4

The right of Davey Winder to be identified as author of
this work has been asserted by him.

British Library Cataloguing-in-Publication Data
A catalogue record for this book is available from the British Library.

10 9 8 7 6 5 4 3 2 1

Edited by Mick Andon
Design by slowcat (*info@slowcat.com*)
Illustrations by Spike Gerrell
Typeset by Pantek Arts Ltd, Maidstone, Kent
Printed and bound by Rotolito Lombarda, Italy

The publishers' policy is to use paper manufactured from sustainable forests.

BUILD YOUR OWN WEBSITE **Contents**

INTRODUCTION 1
What exactly is the internet and the world wide web? Why you should want your own website. What you need to know before you start. What this book will teach you and how to get the best from it. How to go about choosing an internet service provider.

CHAPTER 1 Website basics 7
What is a web page – how is it built and what makes it tick? What exactly is HTML? All you need to know about hyperlinks.
WORKSHOP: Your first web page, p12

CHAPTER 2 Building a great website . . 14
Basic design concepts. The do's and don'ts of website design. Where you can find help with design skills online.

CHAPTER 3 Web authoring software . . 21
Web authoring software tools, and what they can do. How to try before you buy. Free software from Microsoft and Netscape. Compatibility issues.
WORKSHOP: A word processed web page, p25

CHAPTER 4 Layout skills 27
Layout basics. Adding backgrounds. Layout tricks to make your page stand out. Creating lists – ordered and unordered. How to use text fonts and styles effectively. How tables can keep your web page in order. The importance of restraint.
WORKSHOP: Using tables on your page, p32

CHAPTER 5 Navigation 34
How web navigation works, and what options are available. Keeping things neat and easy to use. Navigation bars and indexes. What frames can do for your website, and how to use them wisely.
WORKSHOP: Framing your pages, p38

CHAPTER 6 Adding pictures 40
The pros and cons of adding graphics to your web pages. Different graphic formats. Getting the best results by trial and error. Optimising images for quality and speed. Creating thumbnails. Adding special effects. Interlaced GIFs. Transparent backgrounds. Shadows. Image maps. Image editing software. Where to find pictures on the web.
WORKSHOP: Putting pictures on your pages, p46

CHAPTER 7 Interactivity 48
What is interactivity? The tools you will need. How to add feedback forms to your web pages. Email links. How to run your own chat forum.
WORKSHOP: Adding a guest book to your site, p53

CHAPTER 8 Multimedia 55
Using your imagination, but knowing your limits. Multimedia plug-ins to extend your web browser. Where to find what you need. Streaming audio and video. Video on demand. Where to get media, and how to keep on the right side of the law. Avoiding multimedia overload.
WORKSHOP: Adding sound to your web page, p60

CHAPTER 9 Getting animated 62
Introduction to web-based animation. Do's and don'ts of animated interactivity. How to keep it lean. How to create animated GIFs. Shockwave and Flash plug-ins, Java and JavaScript.
WORKSHOP: Creating an animated banner, p67

CHAPTER 10 Making your website pay . . 69
Advertising: how to sell space on your site. Setting up shop – what to sell and to whom. Shopping baskets, and collecting the money. Making use of a 'middle man'. Practicalities and problems. Tax implications. Where to find the resources you need.
WORKSHOP: Become an Amazon Associate, p75

CHAPTER 11 Getting noticed 76
Promoting your website. Make it easy to find. What makes a 'search friendly' site design? Laying traps for search engine 'spiders'. Active marketing without resorting to junk mail.
WORKSHOP: Search site submission wizard, p80

CHAPTER 12 Publishing your site 82
Duties and responsibilities of a webmaster. Testing and checking your pages and code. Testing with different web browsers. How to upload your files and publish your site. Updating and maintenance. Don't leave anything behind.
WORKSHOP: Publish your first web page, p87

Jargon buster 89

Index 91

About the author
Davey Winder, davey@happygeek.com, is a founder member of The Internet Society of England, a former Technology Journalist of the Year, and author of more than 15 books about the internet. As well as contributing to many computer magazines, including the Computer*active* Web Guide, Davey is an internet consultant who specialises in web usability issues.

Getting started

What exactly is the internet?

Think of hundreds of thousands of computers around the world, connected together by telephone lines, underground and undersea cables, even by satellites in space – and that's the internet in a nutshell. However, this bare essentials explanation doesn't start to do it justice, you have to add the millions of people who actually use it, plus the amazing quantity and diversity of the information it holds and the services it offers to get the real picture. Now the internet becomes more than a sum of its parts, no longer a computer network but a community, a depository of knowledge, an entertainment medium, a place to go shopping and the world's most powerful communications tool.

Historically speaking

To help understand what the internet is today, it's useful to look at its beginnings. The internet was born of a military need back in the 1960s when the US government wanted military scientists to be able to swap information by computer despite the computers and scientists involved being spread all over the country.

The system they developed had to be able to withstand bomb damage, even of the nuclear kind. The solution involved a process where all the computers were linked to each other, and all information sent was broken up into small packets that were delivered separately and then pasted together on arrival.

This way, if one part of the system was destroyed, the information simply hopped from computer to computer to find another way through and arrive safely. Eventually this system moved from military to academic use, and grew until the whole world was using it. The same basic principle is still used to ensure your email and web pages arrive safely at the right destination.

1

Introducing the world wide web

For many people the world wide web is the internet, although it's really just a window onto the net. Just as Microsoft Windows makes using your PC as easy as pointing and clicking with a mouse, so the web brings this usability to the internet. However, behind the simple facade is a very powerful tool. The secret of the web lies in the fact that its pages are interactive, and importantly they are interlinked. Imagine being able to simply touch a word or picture on this page and within seconds see it turn into another page containing related information. Better still, imagine being able to touch the same word and find yourself reading a page from another book in your collection, or even a book from the library, or a library in another city. That's what the web does. What it is, like the internet itself, is just a collection of folders and files stored on thousands of computers (called web servers) around the world. You use a bit of software called a web browser (such as Internet Explorer or Netscape Navigator) to connect to those computers, download a copy of the page in question, and display it on your screen. It really is as simple as that, and by the time you've finished reading this book you will be armed with all the ammunition you need to be able to join in the fun yourself with your very own website.

Father of the web

The web was invented by Tim Berners-Lee, a British programmer who wanted to share ideas and documents between scientists at the European Laboratory for Particle Research in Switzerland. He came up with the idea in 1989, and by 1991 his text-based system was announced to the world. Although popular, it wasn't until 1993, when an American student called Marc Andreesen released the 'Mosaic' browser software with its graphical interface to the web, which soon developed into the Netscape software we all know, that the popularity of the web really exploded.

The Lynx text-based browser gives you an idea what the internet was like in the early days, not the most intuitive of interfaces you will agree.

And the same site, as seen through the eyes of the modern web browser and showing just how far the web has come in a few short years.

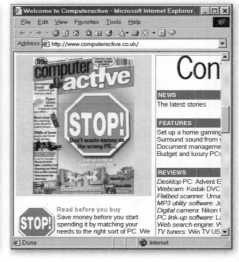

Why do you want a website?

As the web continues to become increasingly popular and visible, with website addresses everywhere you look from television shows to magazine adverts, it is hardly surprising that you will want to get in on the act and have a website of your own. After all it doesn't even have to cost anything; most internet service providers give you enough free space on their web servers, and there are numerous alternative services on the web offering you more free space at the click of a button. You don't even have to buy any special design software to create your pages because the chances are suitable software is already on your computer: FrontPage Express is installed with Internet Explorer and Netscape Composer comes as part of the same package that includes the Navigator browser. Many of the online website services that offer free space for people who want to join their virtual communities also provide simple free tools for creating your pages without leaving your web browser.

So what's the catch?

Surely if it's that easy and that cheap everyone should be doing it? The truth of the matter is that almost everyone is doing it, from the small businesses who can sell such things as sweets, kids' clothes or handicrafts through to the big companies selling flowers, computers, cars and even houses. Others find that the web is the right place for spreading the word about their hobby, or club. Online parish newsletters, details of stamp collections and the most unusual of pastimes such as collecting lunch boxes or photographing electricity pylons all have their place on the web. Then there are the artists who find that a website provides the perfect gallery to display their paintings, poetry or writings to a global audience.

Be it tracing your family tree, providing a virtual tour of your home town or village, or even introducing your pets to the world, if you are going to have a website make it a good one. Make it worthy of the effort you put into creating it and it will be worthy of the time others spend visiting it.

Welcome to
ORPINGTON
PHOTOGRAPHIC SOCIETY

For over 50 years the Society has been one of the leading amateur photographic clubs in the South East of England with a reputation for excellence second to none. Although gaining exhibition and competition successes at local, national, and international level, **the Society's primary objective is to encourage the enjoyment of photography as a hobby, and to enable members to improve their picture making.** New members of all standards – particularly beginners, are always welcome.

The Winter Season comprises weekly meetings from September to May, with a full and varied programme. Additional informal group meetings are held to cater for special interests, And a series of Summer Outings and other social events is also held.

Your website can promote your club, like the Orpington Photographic Society – http://www.opsweb.freeserve.co.uk.

Or perhaps you want to share your love for your pet with the world, like the Guinea Pig Page – http://members.aol.com/cdalziel/cavie.htm.

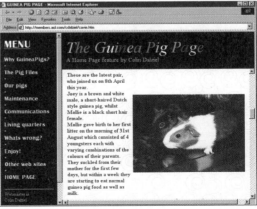

The would-be webmaster

Anyone can become a webmaster or web-mistress, there is no great hidden secret and no apprenticeship to serve. To be good at it is another thing, and requires an understanding of the responsibilities of the job. As webmaster you, and nobody else, are responsible for the planning, design maintenance and marketing of your web pages. The success of your site rests on your shoulders alone, a fact worthy of printing out and attaching to your monitor lest you forget!

Before you start

Before even starting a website design you should ask yourself this simple question 'why do I want a website; what is it really for?'. Only continue if you can provide an answer that sounds convincing to your family and friends. If you just want to be a part of the web, that's OK, but make sure your website has a purpose beyond this.

It helps enormously if you are truly passionate about whatever it is you want to create your website around. If you are bored to tears by the subject, matter then what makes you think that visitors to your site will be any more interested than you? A love for a subject, no matter how trivial it may seem, even down to a page about your pet goldfish, will be transferred magically onto the website

Now you can use Yahoo to research your own venture into website building territory — just search for the subject you are interested in and then take a look at the pages already out there.

and will act as a magnet attracting equally passionate people from around the world to your pages. If you are sceptical, then take one of the biggest and most successful websites there is, Yahoo! This started off as nothing more than an index of the pages that had been visited by two students as they browsed the web. They started compiling the site because they were truly interest-

Yahoo — believe it or not, www.yahoo.com started off as a simple home page project.

ed in sharing details of the places they had been, and the places they had liked, with other internet users. They went on to make hundreds of millions of dollars as a result, but it was a love for the subject matter, not a love for money, that drove them to get started and resulted in them being successful.

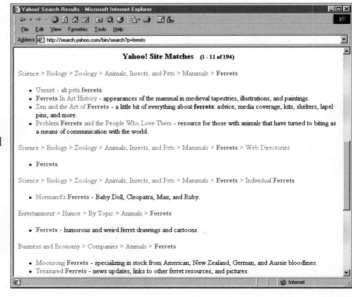

What this book will teach you

We expect that many of our readers will be fairly new to computers and computing, but having said that we know that many of you will already have connections to the internet and be familiar with the basic principles of web browsing. This guide is not meant to be an egg sucking exercise; we will not patronise you but neither will we confuse you with unnecessary technical jargon and geek speak. This book makes very few assumptions about you, the reader, beyond the simple fact that you may want to design and publish your own pages on the web for pleasure or for profit. We will assume that you want to be productive with the technology resources before you, and our intention is to guide you through all the various processes that lead to a successful website.

From beginner to expert

This book is a practical hands-on guide to having a website of your own. It will do this in 12 down-to-earth chapters that will

We will show you where on the web to look for help getting started with your web page design, such as WebMonkey – www.webmonkey.com.

take you from basic concepts through to essential skills, with step by step examples to aid your understanding along the way. Read each chapter in turn, and make sure you fully understand the concepts and examples before moving to the next. The book is structured logically, starting with website basics such as HTML coding and hyperlinks, the glue that holds web pages together, and finishing with a chapter explaining exactly how to get your pages off your PC and onto the web, and maintain them properly once they are there.

And once your website is finished, we'll even offer advice on getting it indexed in those all important search directories such as AltaVista – www.av.com.

In between you will learn:

- essential layout skills such as back grounds, lists, text formatting and tables
- what makes a good page design, and what makes a bad page design
- how to use images on your site without compromising performance and usability
- what web authoring software is available, and which best suits your needs
- how to bring your pages to life using animation and action elements
- the importance of interactivity
- how to make money from the web – the do's and don'ts of making your website pay
- how to bring music, video and other multimedia techniques into your web pages

How to get the best from this book

Reading this book will not turn you into an expert web designer overnight; that only comes with experience. However, we do hope to provide you with the confidence and know-how that will enable you to get out there and get started learning the ropes. Think of us as a trusted friend, offering insight and support whilst you make your first leap onto the web publishing ladder. As well as the will to learn and a reason for wanting a website, you will also need the following items to get the best from this book:

● A graphical web browser such as Microsoft Internet Explorer or Netscape Navigator, which will enable you to browse the web and view existing pages but also let you view your own pages before you publish them on the web. These browsers also come complete with web authoring software which you can use to create your pages, or you can use one of the other software options detailed in Chapter 3.

● An account with an internet service provider (also known as an ISP) to enable you to access the Internet and provide the necessary computer space to publish your pages on the web.

● Enough time to fully absorb the information on these pages, and to try the examples out for yourself. It is only by rolling your virtual sleeves up and getting stuck in that your website building skills will develop.

Choosing an internet service provider

The right internet service provider (ISP) is an essential element of your website project – it will supply you with the physical space on a computer that stores websites and delivers web pages across the internet when requested by visitors. You should ask how much space you will get and how much it

You'll need an internet service provider – but even that doesn't have to cost you money if you use a free ISP such as FreeUK – www.freeuk.com.

will cost. Acceptable answers would be 'at least 5Mb' (preferably 10Mb) and 'nothing', respectively. You should also consider what website address your service provider will offer – avoiding those addresses that include numbers or unusual symbols such as '~'. The best bets are addresses such as www.yoursite.freeserve.co.uk, simply because they are easy to remember, both for you and for your prospective visitors.

A web browser such as Internet Explorer is a necessity, and for good measure it also comes complete with a decent web page creation tool!

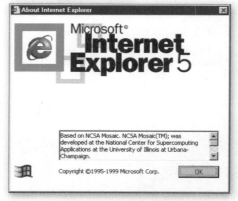

CHAPTER 1

Website basics

What is a web page?

A web page may look like a glossy magazine page, albeit with added interactivity, but they are really very different beasts under the surface. The magazine page is created using desktop publishing (DTP) software that takes all the necessary elements, the formatted text and the pictures, and carefully positions them on a single page, stored in a single file. When this file is opened in the DTP software it is displayed as the designer intended. However, if you open it in another DTP package it will come out looking very different. If you were to load the file into a text editor all you would see is complicated computer programming code. A web page, however, is nothing more complicated than a plain text document, a set of written instructions telling any web browser where all the elements of the page can be located, how to format text, when to include pictures and so on. The text seen on a web page may be stored in one file and the pictures in another, rather than ready formatted and laid out in the same file as with the magazine DTP page. No matter which web browser software you use to view the web page it will be displayed pretty much as the designer intended because all web browsers understand the instructions contained within it. Open the page in a text editor and whilst you may not understand all that you see at this stage in your web designing career, at least you will be able to read it.

Every colourful web page hides plain text behind the scenes – even ours!

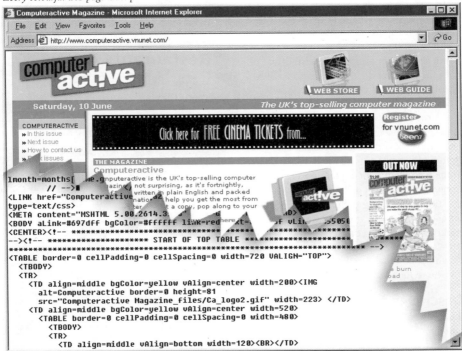

Website mechanics explained

OK, so it's clear that a web page is actually just a collection of files together with a set of instructions that enable your browser to display them pretty much as the designer intended. A website, on the other hand, is simply a collection of web pages that are linked together to enable the visitor to navi-

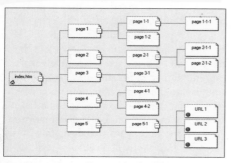

A website is just a collection of individual web pages, all linked together, and stored on a computer that is connected to the internet.

gate from one page to another at the click of a mouse button. Think of the website as being a folder on a computer hard drive, with the pages being sub-folders and files stored within it. If you wanted to view a particular web page you would ask your web browser software to display it. What actually happens is that the browser, connected via the internet, locates the computer holding the website folder and asks to look at the web document containing the instructions for the page in question. It downloads this document along with any graphics that are mentioned in it, from the website computer to your home computer. Once your browser has all the elements of the web page downloaded it can lay them out on screen for you to look at.

Describing the page

The web page document itself doesn't dictate the precise layout or formatting of the finished page, like the DTP document we

mentioned earlier. Instead it defines the elements that go into making up the page, defining the composition not the exact appearance. This means that as the document can be kept fairly small in size it downloads faster and the page appears in your browser window more quickly.

Your web browser software interprets the instructions it receives and then displays the web page as it thinks best. The big advantage is that all web pages should display in all web browsers, irrelevant of what computer system they are running on. The disadvantage is that the same page can look one way when displayed in Internet Explorer and very different in Netscape Navigator. The best websites keep their pages relatively simple so that they will be displayed in all browsers without too much variation. You should bear this in mind when designing your web pages!

What is HTML?

We have established that a web page is nothing more than a collection of files and a set of instructions to piece them altogether, so where does HTML (HyperText Markup Language) enter the equation? Simple! HTML is the code that is used to make up those instructions. Think of it as being the skeleton inside the web page you see – without the HTML bare bones none of the text, images, sound, video or anything else that makes up the flesh of a page could exist. Web pages would all fall apart into an unsightly mess.

HTML is what is known as a markup language. It marks up information in a document, controlling how that information should be seen on screen. Because it isn't a programming language as such, it is much easier to learn – you certainly don't need to be a maths wizard or a computer programmer to be able to write web pages using HTML. It works by using what it calls 'tags' to perform the task of marking up. These are simply letters or words typed between two brackets like this ‹tagname›. Placing an opening tag in front of something in your document tells the web browser how to handle whatever follows, and a closing tag tells it when to stop. A closing tag is the same as an opening one, but has a forward slash in front of it. Together, these two tags are known as a tag pair, and are best thought of as being a sort of 'on and off' shorthand for web page design. So, for example, if you wanted the word 'banana' to be in bold you would do it using the tag pair ‹b› and ‹/b› and the HTML code for that would look like this:

```
<b>banana</b>
```

HTML is a great language to learn because it isn't as complicated as 'proper' computer programming languages. Obviously if you want a complicated web page that means more complex coding behind the scenes but the example at the end of this chapter shows you just how simple it can be, so don't be afraid to try it yourself.

Websites such as Bare Bones – http://werbach.com/barebones are excellent for helping the newcomer to web design understand that little bit more about HTML coding.

The Bare Bones Guide to HTML lists every official HTML tag in common usage, plus Netscape and Microsoft extensions. Version 4.0 of the Guide is designed to conform to the HTML 4.0 specification. For official information on the development of HTML, see the World Wide Web Consortium's HTML activity statement.

I regret that, due to time constraints, I'm no longer able to answer individual questions about HTML or Web design. The resources listed in the left-hand column should address the most common questions.

HyperText Markup Language
Home Page

This is W3C's home page for HTML. Here you will find pointers to our specifications for HTML, guidelines on how to use HTML to the best effect, and pointers to related work at W3C. When W3C decides to become involved in an area of Web technology or policy, it initiates an activity in that area. HTML is one of many Activities currently being pursued.

public drafts | tutorials | guidelines | validation | working group | XForms | forums | HTML Tidy | re| work | html 3.2/2.0 | historical

If you want the full blown technical lowdown on HTML, then turn to the people who invented it, at W3C – www.w3.org/MarkUp.

The links effect

Links, or hyperlinks to give them their correct name, are the strands that weave the world wide web together – connecting page to page, site to site, all at the click of a mouse button. If you have ever used Windows Help then you'll already be familiar with the concept of this information linking, known as hypertext. Clicking on a subject link takes you to another screen with further information where you can click on another link and delve deeper into the help offered. So it is with web pages, except that when you click on a link you may be taken to a different part of the same document, to another page on the same website or even to a page on a different website that could be located anywhere on the planet. The main thing is that a single point and click action will transport you to relevant information, no matter where it is actually stored – content, not location, gets priority on the web.

Jump to attention

Hyperlinks are what bring web pages alive, providing the interactivity that we all associate with the internet. A link can connect you to anything, anywhere, provided that it has a valid internet address. This address is usually referred to as an URL (Uniform Resource Locator), and it simply pinpoints the exact

location on the internet of any given resource. Every web page has its own unique URL. You will find Computer*active* and nobody else at http://www.Computeractive.co.uk for example. But it's not only web pages that can be addressed in this way, so a web page can link to a Usenet newsgroup

A list of newspaper names, but click on one with your mouse and you are transported to their website – thanks to the wonder of the hyperlink.

or a file to be downloaded just as easily. Links are usually underlined words that appear in a different colour to other text on screen so you know where they are, and they change to a different colour after you click on them so you know you've already been there. Pictures can also be used as hyperlinks, and it is even possible to divide one picture up into different areas, known as an image map, each taking you to a different location.

This map is actually an image map – click on any *the states and hidden links take you to that web pa* *You can try it for yourself at* *http://uswebfinder.com/home.cfm*

The learning curve

OK, so by now you should have come to the conclusion that web pages aren't really rocket science, and the thought of creating your very own website shouldn't fill you with dread. There is nothing intimidating about HTML, in fact all that is really involved in learning how to code in HTML is knowing what tags are available to be used, and understanding when to use them and when not to. The learning curve isn't particularly steep, and nobody really expects anyone to be able to recite hundreds of tags parrot fashion. Indeed, when there are plenty of web pages out there that have gone to the trouble of listing all the HTML tags and explaining exactly what each one means in plain English, along with usage guidelines, why should you bother? You should visit WebMonkey (www.webmonkey.com) for an easy to follow HTML cheatsheet, and a tutorial just for kids who want to design their own web pages.

In our hands-on example at the end of this chapter, we show you how to use sim-ple HTML code to produce a rudimentary web page. What's more, we show you how to do this using nothing other than good old Windows Notepad.

This is purely as an exercise to illustrate how HTML works; only the most masochistic of beginners and highly skilled old hands would use something like Notepad to produce a whole website. If the thought of learning all these coded tags and having to type them onto a blank screen sounds a little too much like real computer programming to you, then don't worry, there are other options. You could take the easy route to designing your website, like so many others have done before you, and make use of dedicated web design software packages. These still use HTML code to create the pages, but hide it from the user in the same way a word processor hides all the formatting codes and lets you get on with bashing the keyboard to produce your documents. We will take a close look at the software options in Chapter 3.

The WebMonkey cheatsheet helps flatten the HTML learning curve – find it at http://hotwired.lycos.com/webmonkey/reference/html_cheatsheet

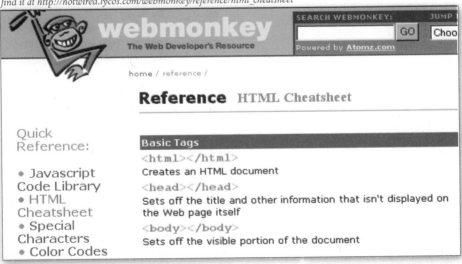

Your first web page - step by step

To show you just how easy using HTML can be, we are going to produce a very basic but nonetheless functional web page using nothing more complicated than Windows Notepad and a little of your time. We suggest you follow our example step by step to get the most from this lesson.

1 Start Notepad by clicking on the 'Start' button and then moving first to 'Programs' and then to the 'Accessories' menu where the Notepad icon is situated. You will be presented with an empty page, or a blank canvas as we prefer to think of it. All web pages start with a declaration that states 'I am an HTML document' to any software that looks at it. This is accomplished by the use of the <HTML> tags within which everything else is located.

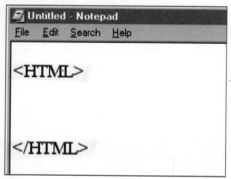

2 The next essential parts of even the most simple web page structure are the <HEAD> tags which in turn contain the <TITLE> tags that determine what

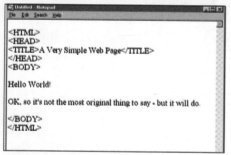

appears in the browser title bar when your page is displayed. Then come the <BODY> tags; everything between these will be displayed in the web browser window when you view the page.

3 Save this file as an HTML document by using the 'save as' option and naming the file with a '.htm' extension, simplepage.htm for example. Now if you load the file into Internet Explorer (File|Open and then browse to where you saved the file) you will see our progress so far. Note the name in the title bar at the top of the browser window. Keep the web browser open, we will come back again and check on progress shortly.

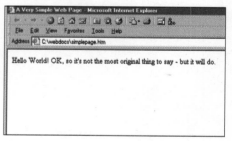

4 Back in Notepad and we can start to jazz things up a little by making our 'Hello World' line into a heading user the header tags. These come in three sizes, <H1>, <H2> and <H3> and you can experiment to see which you prefer. We have also introduced some background colour by adding the BGCOLOR (note the American spelling, it's important) element to the <Body> tag.

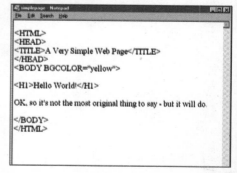

5 Click on the Reload button in Internet Explorer and you can see what a big difference adding a header tag and a background colour element to our code has made. Next we will move the position of the text on the page and make it a little more attractive on the eye.

6 This is accomplished by using the ALIGN element. In this case we've opted for a 'center' justification (again, note the American spelling) together with a horizontal rule <HR> to separate the page heading from the rest of the text. The WIDTH percentage element can be used to determine the length of the line displayed. To position the remaining text we have used the ALIGN element in conjunction with a paragraph tag <P>. Note that this is one of the few tags that doesn't need a closing tag to work properly.

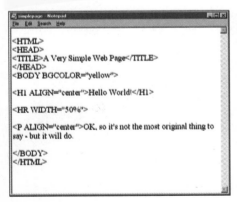

7 Finally for this exercise we will add a picture to the page. To keep things simple we have copied a picture called 'smee.jpg' to the same folder that the HTML file itself is stored in. The <IMG SRC> tag is used to tell the browser where the picture file can be found, and <P ALIGN> can be used to position it on the page. It is also good practice to add a label describing the picture using the <ALT> tag which will display on screen whilst the picture is loading.

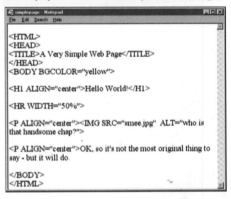

8 And there we have it, a simple but acceptable web page using just Windows Notepad and the most basic of HTML coding. What's more, it only took five minutes to create. Keep reading and we'll show you how to add interactivity and enhance the design so that you can create truly impressive web pages with just as little effort and fuss.

CHAPTER 2

Building a great websit

Basic design concepts

There are two rules of thumb that apply to the web today:

1 people with limited resources of time and money tend to build simple, usable sites.
2 people with an excess of both tend to build complex and user-unfriendly websites.

Somewhere along the line the basic reason for building a website in the first place can get lost in the multimedia overload, the 'cleverness' of the concept and the cutting edge design. Remember that content is still king, people don't visit a website just because it looks good, they want to find something of use to them behind the shiny façade as well. A simple, content-rich, user-friendly design will win out over a complex, content-free, over-indulgent one every time.

This is not to say that your aim should be to produce a flat, text-based page that has minimal interactivity and zero personality. The trick is in knowing how to achieve the right balance between simplicity, usability, individuality, interactivity and technological wizardry. It's not as difficult as it sounds, especially if you take the time to truly think about your website design before you actually start building it. Read through our list of do's and don'ts that follow and absorb the advice before devoting some time to browsing the web. Look for site designs that really appeal to you, and ones that you hate, and then see how the do's and don'ts apply to them in each case. Pretty soon you will be on the right track to understanding the essentials of website design.

Avoid creating a website that appears on the Web Pages That Suck site – www.webpagesthatsuck.com by following some simple common sense advice.

The do's of website design

Do plan your website thoroughly before you start building it. This is a basic principle that cannot and must not be skipped – you wouldn't write a novel without thinking about the plot, the characters, a beginning, middle and ending would you? Ask yourself why you are creating a website, who it is for, what it does and what it won't do. All these are important questions, so don't continue until you have come up with some answers that sound truly convincing.

Do think very carefully about the structure of your website, which pages will contain what information and how they will all link together, how the user will navigate through your content, how you will add new content when it is required. Although this sounds terribly complicated it's actually one of the easiest parts of the design process if you do it properly. By which we mean turning the computer off and getting out an A4 pad of paper and a set of coloured pencils. Each sheet of paper represents a single web page. Mark pages of related content in the same colour, spread the sheets out on the floor and juggle them around to see how they fit together so as to get related information quickly and simply. A paper plan, properly thought through, can save you countless hours of wasted time later when you start to craft your website on the computer.

Do remember that if a user sees text that is black they will read it, if they see text that is blue or underlined they will click on it. If you make all text and links the same colour,

VNUNET – www.vnunet.com establishes an identity straight away, and has a search facility right at the top of the page for ease of use.

There's also a navigation bar that lets you get anywhere on the site quickly.

or underline non-link text, users will not know what to read or where to click for links. The best designs tend to be those that don't fly in the face of accepted conventions such as these.

Do provide obvious and simple navigation tools. A table of contents is essential to any website, be it a navigation frame or a toolbar of links that appears on each page or whatever. So long as the user can see what content is available and where it can be found, he will be happy.

» **M a i n**
VNUNET HOME
SEARCH
Make vnunet.com
your homepage
Privacy statement

» **C h a n n e l s**
THE BUSINESS
THE CONNECTION
THE CHANNEL

» **S e c t i o n s**
NEWS
IN DEPTH
PRODUCTS
FEATURES
RADIO
SKILLS
BOOKS
D*LOADS

» **S i s t e r s i t e s**
ACCOUNTANCY AGE
MARKETING
COMPUTERS
V3.CO.UK
VNU LABS

» **V n u n e t s**
BELGIUM
FRANCE
ITALY
NETHERLANDS
SPAIN

» **J o b w o r l d s**
JOBWORLD UK
BELGIUM
FRANCE

...and more do's

Do put the best content first. Learn a lesson from the magazine publishing industry – there is a reason why they spend so much on front covers – it is to make their publication stand apart from the crowd on the shelf, and to draw the reader in. Your home page, the entry point to your website, should be inviting and informing, it should establish the personality of the site to come.

Do think about download times, as most people will still access your site using a dial-up modem. Design the site to load quickly for them, not for the lucky few with high-speed access. Optimise graphics for web use (see Chapter 6), and keep individual web pages to a reasonable size. Splitting content over three or four fast loading pages is usually preferable to having it all on one slow loading page.

Do pay attention to detail. Check the spelling of all text on all pages before publishing them. Make sure your facts are correct, especially contact details and pricing information if you are selling things. Always read your pages and then read them again; if possible get someone else to read them as well. Tiredness and a lack of time are your worst enemy.

Do add value to your site to differentiate it from the hundreds and thousands of similar offerings on the web. This can come in the way of user interaction, community building, and links to other sites amongst other things (see Chapter 7).

Do have a link back to your home page available from every other page on the site.

Do update your content regularly, especially date-sensitive information.

Do make sure your pages can be viewed in both Internet Explorer and Netscape Navigator before publishing them.

Do remember less is more on the web. White space on the page is your best friend – it costs nothing but adds plenty.

Do include contact details, at the very least an email address, so interested visitors can compliment you on your good design!

News-based sites keep updated to stay in business – don't let your site fall behind the times no matter what it's about.

The internet is all about communicating – so give your readers a way of getting in touch.

The don'ts of website design

Don't forget that you are designing pages for a website, not a magazine, not a CD-ROM, but a website. Think about how many websites have an 'entry tunnel' of slow loading logos or animations, often three or four pages long before you get to the actual site content, and the same thing as an 'exit tunnel' before you leave. This design approach is an accepted norm for CD-ROM presentations, but an alien concept for the web where content is king and attention spans are miniscule.

Don't think that the previous advice means your first page should be a block of boring text – that will drive away the viewer just as quickly as superfluous multimedia. The home page should be welcoming and functional. A graphic is welcoming so long as it isn't so big as to slow down the page loading time. A link into the site or better still a navigation bar of some sort adds the desired functionality.

Don't present visitors with a steep learning curve. The best pages are intuitive, not requiring the installation of obscure plug-in software that the user then has to get to grips with before they can view your web page multimedia presentation. This applies two-fold if the contents of that flashy presentation could have been displayed on screen as easy to use, old fashioned plain text.

Don't 'over-design' your web pages. Tempting as it may be to impose your design skills on the rest of the world, unfortunately the web doesn't work quite like this. If you have read Chapter 1 properly you will know that it is the web browser and not the web designer that ultimately decides exactly how the page appears on the screen. That's why different browsers can display the same page in various ways, and the

more complicated your design the more chances there are of inter-browser incompatibility. Keep it simple, let the HTML mark your documents composition – this is a heading, this is a new paragraph, this is an image, this is a hyperlink – instead of trying to dictate the appearance.

Railtrack (www.railtrack.co.uk) makes good use of white space, establishing their identity and providing navigation and news content all on the quick loading home page.

Waldo's Wallpaper (http://muncaster.com/Tiles.htm) on the other hand has a considerably less welcoming and less informative home page.

...and more don'ts

Don't use an icon to link when a word will do it better. Text has the advantage of being both descriptive and concise, taking up a small amount of screen space but leaving the user in no doubt as to what it does. Only use an icon when it can fulfil the same criteria. It may look good, but if it impedes functionality it has no place on your page.

Don't mix and match or you will succumb to desktop publisher disease. Remember all those awful newsletters with a myriad of typefaces, font sizes, colours and clip art that appeared when DTP software first became affordable? The same thing happens with web design; because it's so easy to add lots of different 'features' to a page, many people mistakenly do so thinking it will produce a good looking page when in fact it does the exact opposite.

Don't be totally self-contained. Links are at the heart of the web, so make the most of them. Visitors will appreciate the added value of links to external websites, providing they are of some relevance. By keeping these links updated and appealing you can create one more reason for people to visit your website on a regular basis. Let the websites you link to know about it, and many will be happy to reciprocate and provide links back to your site from theirs.

Don't 'borrow' someone else's design. There's nothing wrong in using the 'view source' function of your web browser to take a look at the HTML code in order to see how a web page has produced a certain look that you like. However, if you simply cut and paste that code into your own web pages and just change the details to reflect your own site content then you will have stolen someone else's work, over which they hold copyright, and you could certainly be liable for prosecution.

And finally:

Don't litter your website with 'under construction' notices. If a page isn't finished, don't publish it until it is. It's far better to have a single 'coming soon' page detailing your plans than loads of links to nothing at all.

If you do use icons as links, make them obvious and include text where possible, like A2B Travel - www.a2btravel.com

If you are going to produce a fancy multimedia site then offer a plain text alternative like Jessops – www.jessops.com

Learning design skills online

There really is no better way to learn the ropes of website design than by getting out on the web and seeing what others have already done before you. Bookmark sites that you like, and those you hate, so you can refer back to them and see exactly what it is that makes them either so great or so useless. You can also refer to sites that exist solely to help you with your design skills. We suggest you try some of the following:

Great Website Tips (www.unplug.com/great) is divided into sections according to your skill level, and is a real treasure trove of design hints and tips. And just for good measure there's even a section full of links to free web design resources.

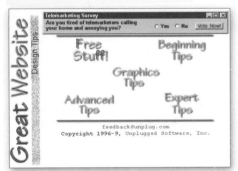

At first glance ProjectCool (www.projectcool.com) is just a collection of links to pages on web design and production. Look beyond this and you'll find an information collective offering all the guidance and inspiration a newcomer to website design could hope for.

At www.pageresource.com/zine/index.html you'll find The Page Resource – another straightforward site which links you to interesting articles aimed at helping you design the very best website you can.

Web Design Tips (www.colin.Mackenzie.org/webdesign) is another slick site full of good advice. You only need to look at this entry page to see that the guy knows his stuff. It's different, it's informative and it loads quickly. Once inside you won't be disappointed either. Load, look and learn!

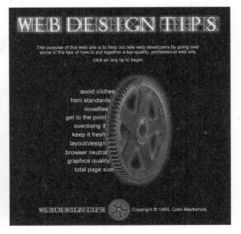

More helpful websites for learners...

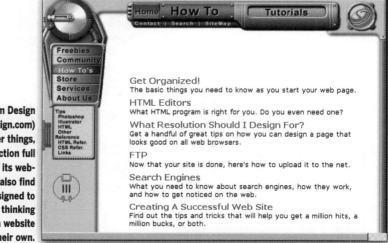

Scream Design (www.screamdesign.com) has, among other things, a very useful section full of 'how to's' on its website. You'll also find plenty of tips designed to help anyone thinking about creating a website of their own.

Get Organized!
The basic things you need to know as you start your web page.

HTML Editors
What HTML program is right for you. Do you even need one?

What Resolution Should I Design For?
Get a handful of great tips on how you can design a page that looks good on all web browsers.

FTP
Now that your site is done, here's how to upload it to the net.

Search Engines
What you need to know about search engines, how they work, and how to get noticed on the web.

Creating A Successful Web Site
Find out the tips and tricks that will help you get a million hits, a million bucks, or both.

Also take a look at Cnet's 'builder' pages (http://builder.cnet.com) for tons of advice and links to online resources for everyone. A good search facility is on hand to help you find exactly what you are looking for.

Check out www.zeldman.com/askdrweb/index.html, alias Ask Dr Web – it's a long established source of online advice, and you'd be nuts not to go take a

Help and Tips for People Who Make Websites.

look at the very least. We'd be very surprised if you don't come away having learned a thing or three.

WebReview (www.webreview.com/pub/design) is another of those must bookmark sites that once you discover you wonder how you could have coped without. Non-patronising but authoritative advice for the website designer.

CHAPTER 3

Web authoring software

What's on offer?

The average would-be website designer isn't that keen on typing a load of pointy brackets, semi-colons and odd sounding tag attributes into a blank screen. Which is where web authoring software comes in. It hides the raw HTML code behind an intuitive graphical interface of toolbars, drag and drop, and mouse clicks that all Windows users are familiar with. The HTML is still there behind the scenes, and you can take a peek at it any time you like, but it really is a lot simpler to hit a toolbar button and select a filename from a drop-down list to insert a hyperlink to another web page than it is to actually sit there and type...

```
<A HREF="document03.html">link
to document 3</A>
```

...more so if your page contains multiple links to references within the same document, to other documents in the same directory and to other web pages on other websites. The name of this game is productivity, and web authoring software provides it in spades. What the software will do for you varies from package to package, but at the very least they will speed up the creation process, remove the need for extensive HTML code knowledge and allow even the novice to prepare professional looking pages after a relatively short amount of time. The more powerful packages will allow you to add complex interactive elements at the touch of a button and take care of administrative and website maintenance tasks such as updating pages and checking links. Which you choose to use will depend upon your needs and your budget.

The latest web authoring tools, such as Microsoft's FrontPage or SoftQuad's HoTMetaL Pro (below), make website design and publishing really easy. The use of preset templates such as this one means that a professional looking page is child's play.

Software options

There are two basic types of web authoring software, the tag editor and the visual editor. Tag editors are nothing more than word processors adapted for web use. Select a passage of text and click on the bold or header button and the program inserts the right HTML tags in the correct place to make things work. The visual editor takes things a step further by letting you work directly in that preview window, providing as near to What You See Is What You Get (WYSIWYG) as is possible in website creation. They hide the HTML code completely, so you only see it if you ask, and bring the art of web page design out of the professional studio and into your front room.

The software selection

The following are some of the major players in the web authoring software business. All prices shown are for guideline purposes only and include VAT. Visit the websites for latest pricing and feature information.
● Adobe GoLive (www.adobe.co.uk) £165
● Adobe PageMill (www.adobe.co.uk) £90
● Allaire HomeSite (www.allaire.com) £75
● Claris HomePage
(www.filemaker.co.uk) £70
● Macromedia Dreamweaver
(www.macromedia.co.uk) £230
● Microsoft FrontPage
(www.microsoft.com) £90
● Namo WebEditor (www.namo.com) £100
● NetObjects Fusion
(www.netobjects.com) £100
● Sausage HotDog (www.sausage.com) £50
● SoftQuad HoTMetaL Pro
(www.softquad.com) £80

Web pages while you wait

There are also a number of services that bundle the whole web building business into one simple package. Just point your web browser at their site and you can sign up for space to host your website and access to the tools to build it. They market themselves as online communities, and their members as virtual 'homesteaders'. These tend to be template driven and web-based, and as a consequence have the advantage of being very easy to use. These two factors are also to their disadvantage; there isn't much scope for flexibility or complexity in the design process, and because it's all done online through your web browser it's not the quickest of tasks either. Take a look at the following services, and the websites already hosted at each, for an idea of what they can offer you:

GeoCities (www.geocities.com)
Tripod (www.tripod.com)

A British, online web service such as Tripod is another method of creating your website, and providing built-in directory and community features. What's more, it's free of charge.

Tripod also provides a web-based home page creation tool that lets you design your site step by step without leaving your web browser.

The no cost option

Actually we lied on the last page, there is a third type of web authoring software – and that's the totally free kind. Leaving aside the Notepad option, if you have installed the latest versions of either the Netscape Navigator or Internet Explorer browser then you will also have their built-in companion design software. Unsurprisingly these are nothing to write home about when compared to the commercially available programs, but then again they cost nothing which is always a plus point.

Microsoft v Netscape

Netscape Composer is the weaker of the two, not having changed much in the years since it first appeared as part of the now defunct Netscape Navigator Gold browser package back in 1996. It can't handle forms, for example, and has an annoying habit of replacing HTML tags it doesn't recognise with silly labels. FrontPage Express is much better, being a cut down version of Microsoft's commercial product. It has been upgraded whenever FrontPage has, and is now quite a powerful editor and one that provides very good value for absolutely no money. It comes packed with templates and wizards to create uniform and impressive page layouts, plus its proprietary 'WebBots' for adding such things as a search engine to your pages at the click of a button. Bear in mind the compatibility warnings on the next page before getting too excited though! As well as your web browser it can be worth checking your word processor or desktop publishing software for web editing options. Take a look at the end of this chapter for an example of web authoring software that you may already have installed on your computer without realising it.

It is also worth visiting the various websites listed on the previous page – as well as evaluation copies of their software many developers also have cut down versions for

home users that are available free of charge. Don't forget to keep an eye on those cover-mount magazine CDs for older editing software that is being given away because a new version has hit the shops.

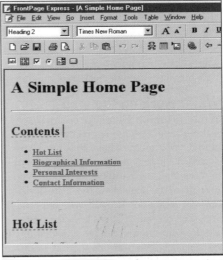

If you can use a word processor, then you can use visual HTML editors like Microsoft FrontPage Express.

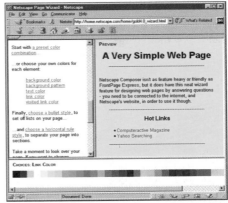

Netscape Composer has an excellent step by step wizard feature that works when you are connected to the Netscape website. Creating pages is just a matter of answering questions and filling in forms.

Buyer beware

Don't expect true What You See Is What You Get (WYSIWYG) functionality from any authoring software, no matter what the box may promise. As we have said over and over again, and will continue to repeat until it sinks home, is that what the viewer actually gets depends which browser they are using, the resolution of their monitor screen, the fonts installed on their PC and so on. There are too many variables to be able to predict exactly how a visitor will experience your website design, no matter what software you have used to create it.

Will it work on the web?

Whilst Microsoft FrontPage is capable of making some very impressive web pages with the minimum of fuss, all is not as rosy as it seems at first glance. The most useful of these interactive extras, the features you can add to the page using the 'WebBot' options, might not actually work once they are up on the web. This is because they require your internet service provider to install special programs on their web computers to effectively enable the WebBots to do their work. Not all ISPs have this option available. You can check for a list of those that have on the Microsoft website, or email your ISP technical support for an answer (and ask if they charge extra for using it whilst you have their attention).

Try before you buy

It's always a good idea to visit the websites of those companies that produce the software and take a look at the exact specifications and functionality there. Look out for any extras that come in the box, things like collections of free clip art, image manipulation tools, a spell checker and ready made page templates and themes to enable even quicker website building. You should also be able to download a trial version of the software before you splash your cash.

Whilst the files may be time-consuming to download, it is far cheaper than buying a product and then realising after a few days that it is either too simple or too complex and so your money is wasted.

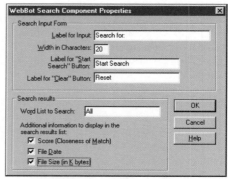

If you want to make use of the very handy Microsoft FrontPage 'WebBots' to easily add complicated extras to your website, then make sure your internet service provider supports them first.

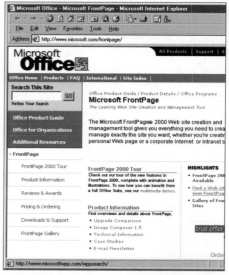

Follow the link from the Microsoft FrontPage website (www.microsoft.com/frontpage) to 'web hosting companies' and you'll find details of the ISPs that support FrontPage's special features.

A word processed web page - step by step

Whilst many web authoring packages look and feel much like a word processor on steroids, some word processors themselves can actually do a pretty good job of creating web pages. One such example is Microsoft Word, and we'll take you step by step through the website creation process using Word 2000 from the Microsoft Office suite.

1 From within Word select the 'New' option from the file menu and then click on the 'Web pages' tab from the window that appears. This comes with a number of templates to make life even easier, but we rather like the web page wizard, so click on that.

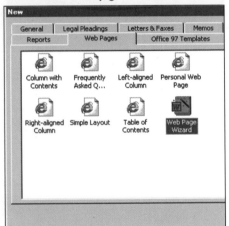

2 When the wizard appears you will be pleasantly surprised to find it really is a very simple and

straightforward piece of software. Just follow the links on the left hand side, in order, and then make your selections from the options offered on the right of the screen.

3 Once you've come up with a name for your site, and a location to store it, the next step is deciding on the general layout. You can choose from two different frames or the separate page approach to navigation. For this example we clicked on the vertical left hand frame option.

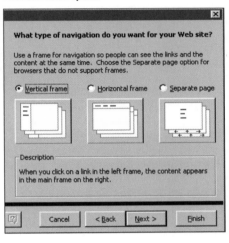

4 As you add pages to the site using the wizard, you can choose from various template sets to save even more time in the design process. Click on an option in the list, and a preview page appears. Once you are happy with a template just click on OK.

A word processed web page, continued

clicking on the Finish button lets the wizard work its magic and open up the web document in Word for you to continue working on.

7 It may look like a fancy word processed document, but it is actually a functioning web page that you can now edit directly from within Word. Notice how the toolbars have changed from normal word processing buttons to web friendly ones.

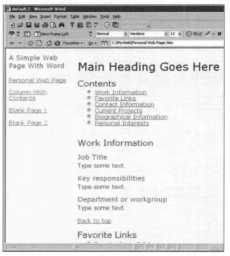

5 After adding pages and organising how they should be ordered, you can move on to the 'visual theme' section which lets you apply a consistent look and feel to all text, banners, buttons, icons, links and so on when they appear on your pages.

6 After just 10 minutes or so of preparation the basic design of our example web page is complete –

8 Editing the web page is no different to editing a letter in Word or any other word processor. You simply select options from menus and toolbars and the tools appear before your very eyes. This is the tool for adding hyperlinks to your page, to link words, images, and so on to other objects or documents.

26

CHAPTER 4 Layout skills

What do we mean by layout skills?

Back in Chapter 2 we looked at the principles of website design, and you might be forgiven for thinking that layout and design are one and the same thing. Actually one leads on from the other. Once you've got your overall site design sorted you then need to concentrate on the layout of the pages that it's made up of. Do you want a plain or brightly coloured background, what about a background image, how should you format the text, how can you control its positioning on the page, what is the best way to break up the monotony of too much text based information, and so on.

We will show you various ways of making the most of your layout skills in the pages that follow, but none is simpler than the horizontal line. Anyone can insert a plain ruled line across a page just by dropping an HTML tag, ‹HR›, at the point on the page where you want it to appear. If you are using a visual HTML editing package you

can literally draw the line on screen as you would in a paint program by dragging the mouse around. The insertion of a line such as this provides a strong visual clue for the reader which reinforces the fact that they are moving from one content area to another. A single line on your web page can make a huge difference to even the most casual of visitors, but too many lines and the page dissolves into disaster. Knowing what to use and when to use it, *that's* layout skill...

Yell (www.yell.co.uk) is a great example of good layout – plenty of white space with good use of colour, plus tables to control positioning of page elements.

Backgrounds

With so much time and effort going into making sure you get the content of your website exactly right, it is all too easy to forget about the canvas upon which you are painting, the page background. Whilst there is a lot to be said for a clean and crisp paper white background, colour when used correctly can make an enormous difference to the look and feel of your pages. In fact it is possible to create an interesting and eye-catching page without the need for excessive images, simply by effectively using background colour.

Stand out, within reason

A strong contrast between background colour and foreground text works best, dark text on a light background is the easiest on the eye, and dark images work best against light backgrounds. If your page has a mix of light and dark text and images then go for complement rather than contrast. Either use a range of colours from the same palette (distinct shades of blue for example) or a

neutral background colour like light grey, as both will show off everything to reasonable effect. Remember it's far easier to change the colour of the background to suit all your graphics than it is to change the colour palettes of your pictures to suit the background. Don't forget that the standard default colour scheme for links in web browsers is blue for unvisited and purple for visited ones, and red when you are holding the mouse cursor over a link. If you want to use a colour scheme that clashes with these, you can specify your own link colours using your HTML authoring software.

Don't be tempted by background images as they seldom work well on the web. They usually interfere with readability of text, add considerably to page loading times, and tiled 'wallpaper' style images look like a dog's dinner. A much better bet would be to use different background colours in table cells, which will result in smaller page sizes and even more impact than if you had used wallpaper images. However, you should remember that the background isn't meant to be in the foreground or it would have a different name so make sure it stays where it belongs by not jazzing it up too much.

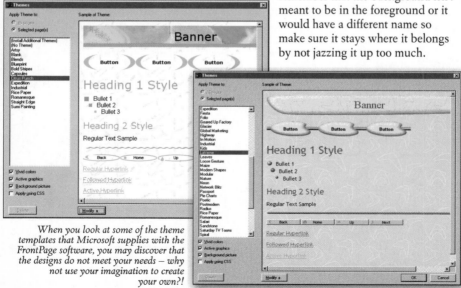

When you look at some of the theme templates that Microsoft supplies with the FrontPage software, you may discover that the designs do not meet your needs – why not use your imagination to create your own?!

Lists

Any web page that reads like a book, with large blocks of text relieved only by the occasional new paragraph here and there, is not likely to be a crowd pleaser. A golden rule of website layout is to use the 'white space' that comes for free on all blank pages. Breaking text up into small chunks is not only easier on the eye, but it also aids usability by enabling the reader to quickly absorb the relevant information from the page. One of the best ways to break up the appearance of text without interrupting its natural flow is to make sensible use of lists.

Ordered or unordered?

There are two basic types of list, ordered and unordered. The only real difference is that an ordered list uses item numbers whilst the unordered one takes the bullet approach. In both cases the adding of consecutive numbers or bullet points is handled automatically by the web browser when it comes across the relevant list tags in the web pages HTML code. The HTML used is very simple indeed; items for inclusion in a list are prefaced with the ‹LI› tag, and all the items themselves are contained between either the ‹OL› or ‹UL› tag pair depending on whether you want ordered or unordered lists displayed. A third type of list is the 'definition list' which is created by prefacing

items with a ‹DD› tag inside a ‹DL› tag pair, These are used to create glossary style lists of terms and definitions, and are therefore specialist in nature and not suited to most layouts. Creating any of these lists in an HTML authoring package is very similar to doing the same thing in a word processor; just click on a toolbar icon and start typing!

How do they do that?

You may wonder, then, what magic codes are needed to get those fancy 3D effect bullets that lists on many web pages feature. Sadly, though, there is no magic involved. The only trickery here is that these are not really lists in the true sense of the word but rather a combination of carefully placed graphic images and paragraphs of text separated by line breaks.

A smart and functional web page. But, whilst the Inland Revenue gives the impression of using lists, actually they are very cleverly disguised tables instead. The giveaway are those fancy bullet graphics.

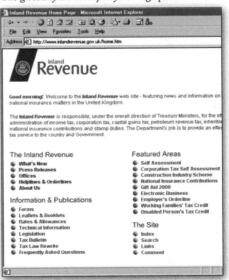

Yahoo News is a shining example of bulleted, unordered lists in action. Boring, maybe, but very functional and fit for the purpose in hand.

Text

Times they aren't a-changing

Web browsers have a font set by default when they are installed, and the vast majority of users won't interfere with this basic Times Roman 12 point setting. It means that most web pages are going to display pretty much as the designer wanted, unless of course the designer has created the pages using a different font. There is an HTML tag, ‹FONT FACE›, that lets you specify any font you fancy on your page, but if the browser of the person who is viewing it doesn't have that font installed it will revert back to Times Roman and so spoil the careful layout of an over-designed page. The naïve web designer sometimes uses specialist fonts thinking that they lift the page, some fake handwriting script or a typeface that is dripping in blood for example. Knowing that the viewer may not have the font in question they include a link to download it from a freeware collection site online, but forget the average visitor isn't going to bother downloading and installing a special font just to read one web page. You can only rely on your viewers having two fonts available to them, Times and Arial/Helvetica. If you absolutely must use a particularly unusual font then make it an image instead of text and that way it will display properly. This will be at the expense of slowing down the loading of your pages, however.

Forms of expression

Basic text styling is limited to formatting codes that turn your typing into bold, italic, underlined and strikethrough – of which only bold is of any real web use. Italicised text can be difficult to read on screen, underlined text is easily confused with a hyperlink (frustrating users when they discover it's not), and anything that has a line through it shouldn't have been on the page in the first place! Neither should you be tempted to centre large blocks of text on the web page – the human brain does not work well when the eye has to keep scanning left and right just to find where each new line begins and ends.

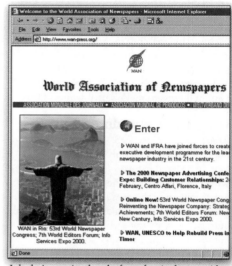

It looks impressive, but the fancy font in the page title is actually a graphic. This is the only safe way to change the typeface in use, and is only viable for small chunks because of the increased size (and therefore time) of the page download.

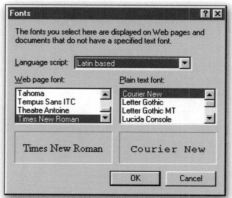

Look in the preferences section of your web browser and you'll find that you can change the default fonts if you like – but be warned that it could mean that some web pages will look odd to say the least.

Tables

Tables are the website designer's friend because they let you take a firm hand over how your pages will appear when viewed across different browsers and using different screen sizes. Similar to the cells you will be used to using in a spreadsheet document, web page tables are equally flexible and easy to use. They let you keep a page neat and tidy, restraining both text and images to a predefined grid of your choosing. You decide how big each cell in this grid is, how many rows and columns form the table, even what colour the individual cell backgrounds are.

Less is more, more or less

Like just about every other aspect of web page design, less is more – so don't get carried away with too many cells, no matter how tempting it may be. The reason in this particular case is that browsers will try to read the whole table before starting to display it, so the bigger the table is, the longer the page takes to load, and we've already established that that's a design disaster area. It is much better to break up your page into several small tables than rely on one big one. And whilst we are talking about table size, now is a good time to mention that you can define the height and width of the overall table by either the number of pixels or as a percentage of the available screen space. Because you don't know what resolution your visitors will be using, it is advisable to avoid fixed pixel measurements and opt for percentages instead. Many people still browse the web using 640 × 480 low resolution monitors, but the average screen size is now commonly thought to be 800 × 600, and many power users are at 1024 × 768 or above. If you specify the width of your table as being 600 pixels then everyone, including those

looking at low resolution screens, will be able to see everything on your page. However, on a high resolution screen it will look very small. If you use the percentage option the table will automatically resize with the browser window, with 100% meaning it will take up all the available window space.

Some sites look like they use tables, when in fact they don't – such as this earthquake page which actually has an imagemap with embedded links instead (www.gsrg.nmh.ac.uk).

However, to the untrained eye others, such as vnunet, don't look like they use tables at all but in fact do.

Using tables on your page - step by step

Tables are very easy to use, and very powerful tools in your design arsenal. Every HTML authoring package will be able to create tables and let you manipulate them to your heart's content. We have used the free Microsoft FrontPage Express software that comes with the Internet Explorer browser in our example, but table creation is almost identical no matter what web design software you use.

1 There are two options for creating tables in FrontPage Express, the toolbar icon which pops up a slightly confusing selection grid, or selecting 'Insert Table' from the Table menu as we have done here.

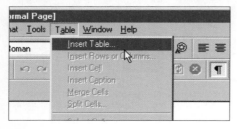

2 A table properties box will now appear, and this enables you to define a number of options, including

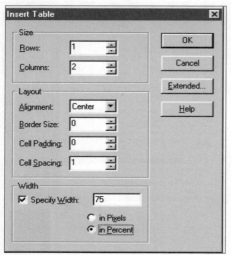

how many rows and columns will initially appear, the table width, and allignment on the page. We have chosen a 2 column, 1 row table, to be aligned in the centre of the page and with a width of 75% of the available window space.

3 This gives us a two cell table at the top of the page, ready for us to start playing with. Right-click over one of the cells and select Cell Properties from the drop down menu.

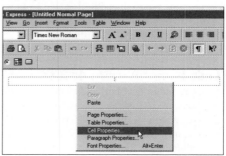

4 You can now split the percentages of the table width between the two cells, handy if you want a text banner in one and a logo in the other, for example. Background colours for each cell can also be selected from a drop-down palette whilst here.

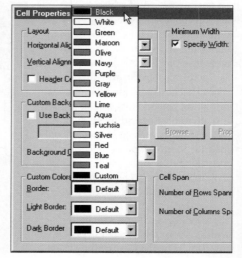

32

5 Click on the cell, and then select 'Image' from the 'Insert' menu at the top of the screen. Browse your image directory for whatever picture you want to display, and our smart page banner table is starting to take shape.

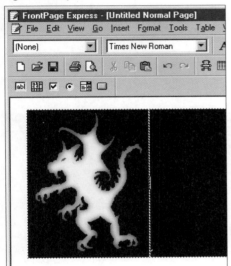

6 Select a contrasting text colour – here we've chosen red to stand out well against the black background. Click on the other cell and type the name of your page. Now you can use the increase text size

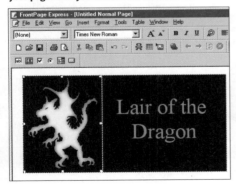

button (large A) to enlarge the title until it fits the table cell to your liking. If your text is too large, adjust it using the decrease text size button (small A).

7 You can insert more rows and columns using the Table menu, make the image into a hyperlink using the Edit|Hyperlink menu, and generally play around until you are happy with your banner. Make sure you save the page before quitting though.

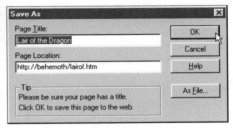

8 And here is what we achieved in less than five minutes using a table to create a very effective page banner. Think what you could do if you devoted an hour or two to the project!

CHAPTER 5

Navigation

Many novice website designers make the mistake of thinking that navigation is a simple process, and one that requires little thought. After all, it's just a matter of plonking a couple of icons on the page saying 'home' and 'back to top' and leaving the rest down to the links embedded on the page, isn't it? Yet scratch the surface and you will soon discover it's a lot more complex than that. If you get the site guide wrong, people won't be able to find the information you have so carefully crafted onto your pages. Nor will they hang around and try and work out where it is hiding. Get it right, on the other hand, and not only will the visitor be able to quickly find the content they need, but they will just as easily pick up on the content they didn't know they needed.

For example, a site with lots of pages that can be viewed in any order is best served by an index frame or navigation bar. A series of sub-pages that only make sense when viewed in order would do better to have one link to get you to the first page and then leave further navigation options to 'back', 'forward' and 'home' arrows only. So navigation should be right up there next to content at the planning stage of your website building project. It's that thing about laying out pieces of paper and discovering the best ways to link them together that we cited as one of the 'do's of website design' way back in Chapter 2.

The Nationwide website (left) offers a good example of most of the navigation elements you'd want from a home page.

1 – Drop down menu
2 – Navigation bar
3 – Navigation bar, text only version
4 – Links to other services
5 – Survey link
6 – Off site searching
7 – Banking link
8 – Featured pages

The Nationwide Building Society manages to create a 'site map' that doesn't look like a table of contents. This page proves that you can index site content easily and quickly without compromising design.

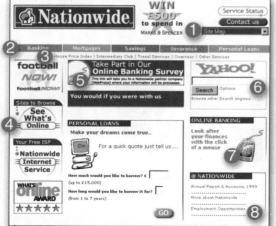

Navigation options

An index page containing links to all the other pages on the site has the advantage of being just about the simplest kind of navigation system to create; it's just another web page after all. Whilst it can look good, and if it's the entry page to your website you know that people are going to see it, there are some obvious problems. First, as soon as your visitors navigate to another page the index disappears. They can get back to it by hitting the back button on the browser or the index link that you've thoughtfully included on each page but it adds a layer of annoyance to the user experience.

Index it

A better bet is to create an index that loads on every page on your site, so that it is always available for reference. This would be a cumbersome and space-consuming exercise if you used the same kind of list of links already mentioned. Better to use a navigation bar, a set of images stacked on top of each other to give the appearance of a single strip of labelled menu buttons. Each image is actually also a link; one click and the user is on the right page. Use the same piece of HTML code on each page on your site and the bar will appear on all pages and in the same place. This does add an over-

head to page loading times, however, so you can take the next step forward and make the navigation bar a single image that has various link hotspots within it. It looks and acts just like the bar of separate images, but is smaller and quicker to load. The hotspots are achieved by making use of something called an image map, which can be created easily by your web authoring software or web graphics software. This allows you to lay an invisible grid over the image and allocate different links to different parts of the image.

Place a navigation bar inside a frame (see next page) and it looks good, increases usability, and saves visitors time by not forcing the browser to reload it every time they move from page to page.

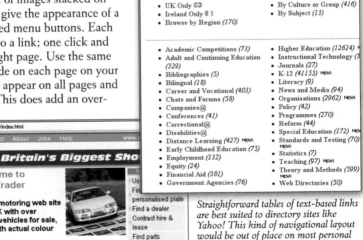

Straightforward tables of text-based links are best suited to directory sites like Yahoo! This kind of navigational layout would be out of place on most personal home pages.

Auto Trader have given a lot of thought to getting around this big site. The navigation bar stays put on the left and features a drop-down menu to get straight where you want to go.

In the frame

So what is a 'frame' exactly? Frames can probably be best explained if you think of the web page that is displayed inside your browser as being a window made up of a number of panes. Each pane is in fact a totally separate web page, each containing its own set of text and images held together by HTML code. Holding all this together is something called a 'frameset', more HTML code that defines how big each of the panes are and which web pages should be loaded into which frame – it's almost like a big frame that stops the rest from spilling over the screen. The important point about frames is that you if you use them properly you get to control their size, position and content which not only helps the navigation of your website, but also its overall look and feel as well. When implemented with care and attention they can add considerably to the professional image of your website. Use without proper thought and your pages become all but unusable.

```html
<html>

<head>
<meta http-equiv="Content-Type" content="text/html;
charset=windows-1252">
<title>New Page 2</title>
<meta name="GENERATOR" content="Microsoft FrontPage 4.0">
<meta name="ProgId" content="FrontPage.Editor.Document">
</head>

<frameset rows="64,*">
  <frame name="banner" scrolling="no" noresize
  target="contents" src="red.htm">
  <frameset cols="250,*">
    <frame name="contents" target="main" src="blue.htm">
    <frame name="main" src="yellow.htm">
  </frameset>
  <noframes>
  <body>
  <p>If your browser doesn't support frames, please
  click <a href="index.htm"> here</a></p>
  </body>
  </noframes>
</frameset>

</html>
```

The highlighted HTML code is the 'frameset' that instructs the web browser where each frame should go and what web page each should display.

And here's what that particular example frameset looks like when displayed out of the HTML editor and in the web browser.

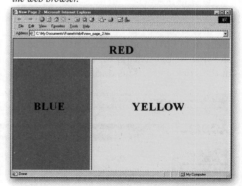

Keep it neat

It is very easy to have lots of frames on your web page, however, it's not a good idea to overdo it. First, the more frames you have on a page the messier the design can look. Second, and perhaps more importantly, every frame included is yet one more thing to download. A navigation frame and a banner/logo frame save on overall download times because, as we've already mentioned, they are static. Yet every additional frame is really just another web page, albeit a small one, that adds to the overall amount of information to be downloaded. A three frame layout is generally accepted as being the largest you should look at: any more and you are in danger of slowing down initial page loading times to the point where a user goes elsewhere. The best 'framed' websites are nearly always the ones where you don't even realise they are using them.

Pros and cons of using frames

A typical frame-enabled website would see the page divided into two or three frames, in essence separate web pages contained inside the one browser window and displayed as a single page. A vertical frame (1) extending up the entire left hand side of the page could contain an index of all the pages on the website, with maybe a small but wide frame (2) at the top of the screen acting as a branding banner and holding the company name and logo, and finally a large frame (3) taking up the remainder of the screen. Frames 1 and 2 remain static and constant, but frame 3 changes to display the pages as selected by the user when they click on a link listed in frame 1. It doesn't take a genius to work out that this structure can make a website not only easy to navigate, but also easy on the eye. Frames bring consistency to your pages, and increased usability thanks to establishing a 'look and feel' across the whole site.

Frame overload

On the downside comes the fact that too many frames spoil the browser, and older versions of web browsers won't support them at all so you risk making your site unreadable to a proportion of visitors. One of the most common problems with framed websites is that there is a tendency to confuse search engines when it comes to indexing your site properly. The problem lies with the fact that these sites send software robots called 'spiders' to crawl around the web looking for new pages to index in the search database. If they come across a poorly framed site they may only see the 'frameset' code and not all the pages contained within, so the bulk of your website could get left out of the search

engine database. The solution to getting listed on these sites, and therefore ensuring that would-be visitors can find you in the first place, is to add some HTML ‹noframes› tags after all the frame code (see the step by step example for more on this). This is where you can describe what content is contained within the framed pages. It has the advantage of allowing older browsers to be able to see into your website as well.

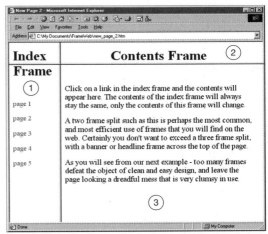

When using frames, the simple approach is often the best.

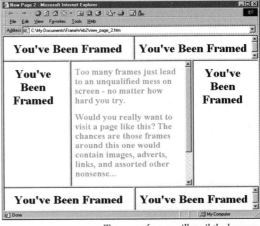

Too many frames will spoil the browser.

Framing your pages - step by step

Adding frames to your website design is actually pretty easy when you use any of the WYSIWIG HTML authoring software. We have used Microsoft FrontPage for this example, but most of the programs function in much the same way, so apply the same basic principles and you'll come up trumps.

1 Select 'New Page' from the File menu and click on the 'Frames Pages' tab to get a selection of frame templates to choose from. As you select a different template, the layout appears in the preview screen to the right. We have opted for 'Banner and Contents' which is a standard three pane design.

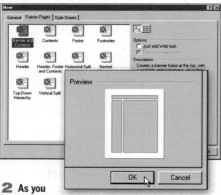

2 As you can see, the basic frames layout now appears in the editing window, complete with a button in each pane. You can either click on 'Set Initial Page' to

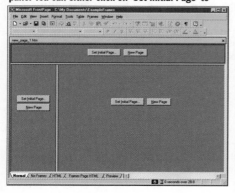

choose a web page you have already created, or the 'New Page' button to create brand new content for each frame in your set.

3 We chose a new page for each frame, and this is what you get – three blank canvases to work on. You can resize the frames to suit your design simply by dragging the frame borders, as you would expect. This automatically adapts the underlying HTML code to reflect your changes.

4 You can now work on each frame as a separate web page, as you would if it were a standalone page because essentially that's what it is. Right-click over a frame and select 'page properties' to alter backgrounds, text, link colours and so on for example.

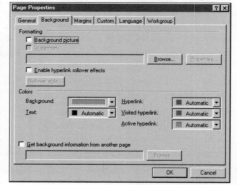

5 Because this example is purely a tutorial concerning the creation of frames we won't worry too much about the content. However, we have changed the background colour and added some descriptive text so as to illustrate that each frame is a separate page. This is what our framed page looks like now.

6 Right-click over a frame and select 'Frame Properties' to fine-tune such things as the visibility of scroll bars. If a page is too large to be displayed in the frame when viewed by a visitor's web browser then scroll bars can be added. Use the 'if needed' option to add them only when required. The 'resiz-

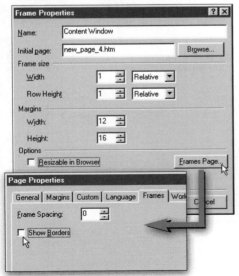

able' option lets people change the frame size in their browser and clicking on 'Frames Page' lets you turn off frame borders so no dividing lines are seen between frames.

7 Clicking on the 'Frames Page HTML' tab shows you the frameset code, and lets you replace the unhelpful message that we've highlighted with something more user friendly like "If your browser doesn't support frames, please click here". Highlight the text then click on the 'No Frames' tab so you can edit this section of code and make the word 'here' into a link pointing at a non-framed index page.

8 Save your work and you can view it with Internet Explorer. Note there are no borders, no scroll bars, and nothing that would make you think it was a framed page if you took the colour coding element away. OK, so this was a very quick lesson in frame building, but we hope it has shown there is little to be scared of when it comes to increasing the usability of your website with frames.

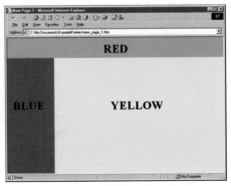

CHAPTER 6

Adding pictures

Introducing images

If there is one thing that will prompt endless debate amongst website designers and users, it would be the thorny subject of web page graphics. Some people hate them so much that they actually use the 'no images' option in their web browser software so that they aren't downloaded at all. This undoubtedly speeds up the web browsing process, but it also provides plenty of ammunition for the pro picture fraternity. Most web pages are designed using images of some description or other, so take them out of the equation and the page tends to fall flat. Design a page from scratch without any graphical elements and the same thing happens, but on all browser screens. The honest truth is that without graphics most web pages will look bland at best and monotonous at worst.

Too much of a good thing?

So why is there any debate over the use of images at all, you may be asking yourself? Simple, the 'world wide wait' syndrome which has us twiddling our thumbs whilst waiting for a web page to download and appear in our browser is made worse by poor use of graphics. Too many on the page, file sizes that are too big, images are used when text would do the same job but much faster... these are all to blame. It is true to say that pictures really can make a good site or break a bad one. Avoiding the many pitfalls is essential if your website is to fall into the first camp rather than the latter,

so read on and absorb the arty advice that we are about to offer.

FREE GRAPHICS
we know where the good stuff is

exclusive offer

01 Web Graphics Categories:

ClipArt
Straying from the standard buttons and bullets, these are more cartoon like pieces great for spot illustrations.
(17 links)

Control Panels
Control panels are larger images which are usually customized as image maps -- usually high-tech looking.
(12 links)

Families Themes Sets
Matching backgrounds, buttons, bullets, etc. to give your site a nice consistent look -- which makes navigation easier for your surfer and gives you a much stronger web presence.
(58 links)

Misc BBB
Miscellaneous buttons, bullets, bars, etc. Not usually matching sets.
(30 links)

If you don't want to, or can't, produce your own web graphics there are plenty of websites such as Free Graphic (http://www.freegraphics.com) who can provide them ready made and free of charge.

Graphic formats

There are two main graphic formats used in web design, GIF (Graphics Interchange Format) and JPEG (Joint Photographic Experts Group). GIF images have no more than 256 colours, whereas JPEG images have a rather impressive 16,777,216 colours. So straight away this tells us that GIFs are better for small images such as icons or clipart which don't have that many colours in the picture, and JPEGs are more suited to larger, complex pictures with lots of colour information, such as photographs. This also suggests that the different formats will be different sizes as well, which indeed is the case. GIFs offer savings in file size because there is less information to store, JPEGs are bigger and so take longer to download but make use of compression techniques to keep file sizes down to acceptable levels for web use. Using GIFs as much as possible makes for a quicker to load page, and is to be recommended. Only use JPEG images when you need extra colour, for displaying photographs, for example.

Trial and error

There is no hard and fast rule about using the two formats though, and often it can be worthwhile experimenting a little. You can save the picture as a JPEG image and then convert it to 256 colours in your graphics software and save it as a GIF file. Drop first one into the page and load it into a browser and then the other, and choose the one which provides the best balance between appearance on the page and time taken to download. Remember to factor in the number of other images that will be on the finished page when considering download times though, as they have a cumulative effect on loading speed. A useful tip is that you can make JPEG files smaller by choosing to save with a 'high compression' option. This removes some of the information from the saved image. The higher the

compression the more information is removed, so the smaller the file becomes. The downside is that quality obviously suffers, so it's a matter of balance once again.

This image of the author is saved in JPEG format using the lowest compression for best quality. It is a hefty 109Kb in size.

The same image, this time saved as a 16 colour GIF format image, which brings the file size down to just 18Kb, but it badly affects the quality.

And for the last time, saved as a 256 colour GIF format image, providing acceptable quality and acceptable size at just 38Kb.

Optimising images for web use

We have already seen how the format in which you save your image files can impact upon the quality of the graphics as they appear on the web page, and how fast they load into a visitor's browser screen when they download your page. This is just part of a process known as web optimisation, and is a vital element to any successful web-site design. Much of this optimisation could also be grouped together under the heading of common sense preparation, but still far too many people seem to throw the ability to think straight out of the window in their headlong rush to get pages out there and published as soon as possible. A little time spent tinkering in some graphics software is a great investment though, and one which you should make without exception. Here are our top tips for making the most of your web page images.

Cut out excess fat

First always cut away any excess using your image software's cropping tool. This is akin to taking a pair of scissors to a photograph and cutting out the bit which has your uncle's leg and the dog in it, leaving just the smiling face of your aunt. Size is a key issue for web page images, so don't make them bigger than they need to be by leaving any rubbish in the frame. Similarly, cut away any of the background that is not needed. This saves space and produces an image that will have more impact on your page.

Rule of thumb

If you want to make larger images available to those who don't mind the wait then use thumbnails, small versions of the image that link to the full-size original. Resize the image to just 100 pixels width and save under a new file name. Use this image to display on the web page, and make it a hyperlink to the big image so that when a user clicks on the thumbnail it will down-

load and display. If you have a lot of thumbnails to display, the easiest method is to put them in a table (see Chapter 4) so you can present them properly spaced.

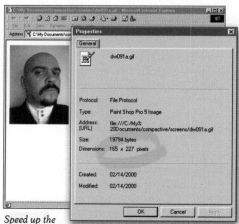

Speed up the loading of your images into the web browser by telling it how big the picture is in advance. Note the size and add this to your HTML code after the ‹IMG SRC="images/picture.gif"› bit so it ends up looking something like:
‹IMG SRC="images/picture.gif" WIDTH="165" HEIGHT ="227"›.

Use free software like the GIFCruncher and JPEGCruncher at http://www.spinwave.com to squeeze every last bit of excess size out of your images.

The right effect

Computers and graphics were made for each other. Once an image is inside your PC it is just a bunch of pixels on the screen, digital data ready to be manipulated. And you can manipulate it to your heart's content and produce some worthwhile effects suited to web usage, all without breaking sweat by using your favourite image editing software.

Layer by layer

Let's start with interlaced GIFs, which really aren't as complicated as they sound. All interlaced means in this instance is that the image is built up of multiple layers of lines, so that the whole image can be displayed without all the lines intact before the entire image file has been downloaded. What this means in practice is that the user can see what the image is going to look like without having to wait for the whole thing to download before it is displayed. Interlacing adds a little to the overall file size, but it also adds to the usability of your web page by enabling the picture to be seen more quickly. To create an interlaced GIF simply select GIF as the 'Save as' type and ensure the 'interlaced' option is set. It's as simple as that.

Invisible colours

Transparent GIFs are also useful, since they allow you to make part of the image invisible when viewed in the web browser. What use is that? Well, say you create a logo on a white page. You can simply drop this onto a web page with a white background and the logo blends in perfectly. But if you wanted to drop it onto a black background you've got serious problems. Which is where the transparency comes in; you just make the white background of the logo invisible so that it can be blended into any page you fancy as it lets the web page background show through. The method of doing this will vary from program to program, but in Paint Shop Pro – one of the most popular image editors – for example, you select 'Set palette transparency' from the Colours menu and simply click on the image to choose the colour to make transparent.

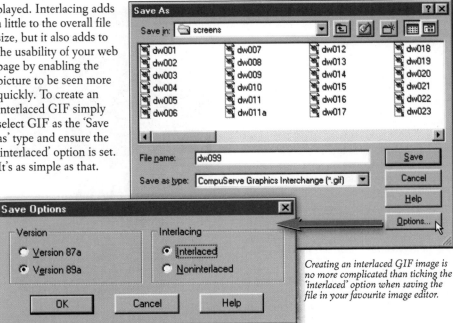

Creating an interlaced GIF image is no more complicated than ticking the 'interlaced' option when saving the file in your favourite image editor.

43

The right effect (continued)

So far we have concentrated on making your graphics user-friendly rather than exciting, but there is no reason why they can't be both. Let's face it, bland images are worse than no images; they take longer to download for a start. So what are your options for getting a little creative with the pictures on your pages?

Casting shadows

Drop shadows involve a little more work on your behalf than either interlacing or transparency, but the effect is pretty impressive if you do it right (which means, you've guessed it, not overdoing it on the page). What a drop shadow does is cast a shadow falling from the image, which produces a

Drop Shadow

Something as simple as a drop shadow effect can make a striking difference to a page title, or anything that you want to really stand out.

kind of 3D look to your graphics. It's a bit more complicated because to get this effect you will need to have more than the 256 colours that a GIF contains. So first you must increase the colour depth of your image to 16 million colours. Then copy the image and make it a 'new selection' and paste it to where you want the shadow to fall. Select 'Drop shadow' from the special effects menu and fiddle with the options until the preview image looks right.

Finally decrease the colour depth back to 256 and save as a GIF again. Again, this varies depending on the image editing software you are using.

Image maps

If you are feeling really adventurous then you might want to consider creating an image map of the type we mentioned briefly in the last chapter when talking about navigation bars. This is best done not in your graphics software but rather in your HTML authoring software, because these tend to have very good specialist imagemap tools built in. Using FrontPage for example, you simply select a suitable image and then use the hotspot buttons on the picture toolbar to map out which bits of the image will act as hyperlinks for your web page. You can also choose from rectangular, circular or polygon shapes to form the image hotspot – which should be enough to suit most people's picture requirements. Then, once you have drawn the hotspot over your image you simply select a web page for it to link to, and that's it done. You can repeat this until the image has all the hotspots and hyperlinks you need – that's really all there is to creating an interactive image map.

The square frames on the tree are the hotspots that turn this clip art into an interactive image map.

Image software

As you will now appreciate, there is a whole host of software that can be used for manipulating the graphical elements of your website. The trick is knowing exactly what you need and what is overkill. Essentially most first time web designers will be able to manage quite well using a combination of an HTML authoring program like the ones we looked at in Chapter 3, plus a basic all-round graphics package such as Paint Shop Pro. If you have deeper pockets and a desire to do that little bit more with your images then dedicated web graphics software such as Adobe ImageStyler and Macromedia Fireworks might appeal. But be warned, there is a learning curve attached to powerful programs such as these, and you may well find them to be a case of overkill unless you expect to be doing a lot of highly graphical web design work.

Use the web

However, you don't have to invest time and money in lots of arty software, you could always let the web help you to help it, by making the most of the free image utilities it offers. These tend to be aimed specifically at one task, and so they do it very well and with the utmost of ease for the user. CoolText (http://www.cooltext.com) will create impressive banner text images for you, for free. Choose the style, choose the font, choose the colour, type in the text, hit a button and within a few seconds your image is ready to download and drop into your own pages. Or how about the equally impressive WebFX (http://newbreedsoftware.com/webfx) which takes the place of all those framing, filtering and animation tools found in most high end graphics software and provides them on the web for free. Enter the address of your web page and WebFX pops up a list of available images there which you can choose to manipulate. Select an image, select a tool, apply it and

the image is converted in a single mouse click. Finally, you should also take a look at the ButtonMaker site (http://www.buttonmaker.com) which enables you to transform any GIF image into a button ready to be used on your web pages.

Take the hard work out of creating professional looking banner text – let someone else do it for you. CoolText is a superb online resource.

WebFX is a special effects web workshop for your images. Take any image on your website and WebFX will transform it into something else altogether.

Putting pictures on your pages

This is the easiest part of dealing with web images. Once you've created or collected a graphic, optimised it for web use, all that's left is to place it on the page. We have used Microsoft FrontPage in our example, but all HTML authoring software works in much the same way when handling images – so follow the basic advice given here and you can't go wrong.

1 A web page without any graphical content can be very effective if well designed, but most will just end up looking very boring indeed, just like our rather sad example.

2 Load your page into the HTML editor, move the cursor to roughly where you want the image to go (we can tidy it up later), and then use the 'Insert|Picture|From file' menu to locate the image in question.

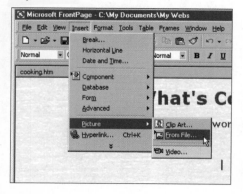

3 The image can be in the same folder as your web page, but it is tidier to keep it in a separate 'graphics' folder along with all your other web images. Anyway, double-click on the right filename and your picture will appear on the page.

4 Right-click over the image and select 'Picture properties' from the drop-down menu so that we can make a few essential adjustments such as adding the alternative text.

5 The alternative text attribute serves several functions. Originally it was just so that people using web browsers that didn't support graphics could still use the page. Now the latest browsers also identify the picture by popping up the text when the mouse cursor is moved over it.

6 Moving to the 'Appearance' tab, you can configure the alignment of any text relative to the image, so it appears above, below, or in the middle. Plus you can specify the image size to speed up loading as explained earlier.

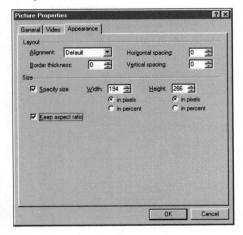

7 Using the hotspot feature we can make the box at the bottom of the image into a hyperlink that takes visitors into the website proper. This turns a plain picture into an interactive image map.

8 This is the same basic page layout that we started with, but now the addition of a simple image has transformed it in terms of both appearance and usability, all in the space of a few minutes.

CHAPTER 7 Interactivity

What is interactivity?

There would be no world wide web without interactivity, that much is obvious, but what is meant by interactivity as it applies to your website? More importantly, what about the individual pages within it? Think of a web page with a navigation bar to one side and hyperlinks that transport you straight to related content, with a button to press that lets you send email to the person who created or publishes the website, and also a search box to find the stuff you are interested in really quickly. This is interactivity, the basic principle of making a visit to your website a two-way experience between the visitor and the content held within the pages.

But if you want to make your website a truly memorable interactive experience you have the option of offering just that little bit more than the bare essentials. How about an area where visitors can discuss issues raised on your website by using a simple chat forum, or giving them the opportunity to fill in a form so that you can add them to a mailing list which will keep them informed about new additions to the site, or even a simple but often appreciated opportunity to sign a guest book and pass comment on how much they liked or disliked your website creating efforts? All this is possible with a little effort on your behalf. Read on and not only will we explain the basics but also show you exactly how to add a guest book to your website.

A guest book like 'Toshi and Jackie's' (www.geocities.com/Tokyo/Ginza/5275) is a simple interactive element, yet it provides both useful feedback for you and a sense of community for the user.

Tara Frohlich	
City:	Saitama, Japan at this time Aust
Email:	None
Words of wisdom:	You computer whiz how did you get this up and running. Great job. Love it!
Favorite Website:	None
Fri Nov 20 10:14:46 1998 EST	

Sally	
City:	Gold Coast Aust
Email:	sallyann@elink.com.au
Words of wisdom:	Best of luck Jackie and Toshi. I hope your lives together are everything you wish for!! Jackie, I'm a friend of your Mum's - Ive met you a few times before. Anyway, I'll be in Japan on Monday the 31st Aug for 5 days so if I get a chance I'll give you a call. I'm staying at the Tokyo Hilton. Hope to catch up with you soon.
Favorite Website:	None
Sat Aug 29 18:17:29 1998 EST	

Toshi & Jackie's Guestbook!

All the information below is optional, except for your name. Please note all information registered in the registry is viewable by anyone.

Thanks for stopping by!

Name:
City:
Email:
Country:
Favorite Website: *http://*
Words of wisdom:

Private Notes (Not displayed in registry):

[Sign Guestbook]   [Clear Form]

Interactive advice

Remember that the content of your site, coupled with ease of use, are the most important things. Interactivity is a part of this, but should not be overdone. A page where every other word is a hyperlink is harder to use than one where hyperlinks are included only where they truly add to the user experience. Similarly, getting visitors to fill in an online form is a great way to get feedback and keep in touch with those who are using your site, but only if they choose to do it. Placing such a form at the top of the first page on your website is a surefire way of ensuring people go no further. Interactivity is not adding a 'hit counter' to your page, proudly displaying the fact that 96 people have visited your website since last Friday. If you want to know how many people are visiting your website, ask your ISP or web hosting company to help. The chances are that they will already have the necessary systems in place to provide you with all the visitor statistics you need.

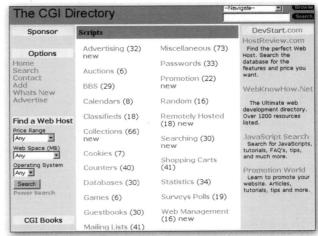

The CGI Directory (http://cgidir.com/Scripts) has hundreds of tools for adding interactivity to your pages. Just make sure your ISP will let you use them before you start any work though!

Tools of the trade

Interactivity can mean making use of special tools, either ones that come with your web authoring software or ones that you can download from websites offering free tools (known as 'CGI-scripts') for creating chat rooms, guest books and so on. These are fine, but talk to your ISP before adding them to check that they will work OK. Lots of ISPs and web hosting companies will charge more money for allowing the use of either FrontPage extensions or running those special scripts. However, there are an increasingly large number of web-based services that offer free interactive elements for your pages. Such things as guest books and discussion forums only involve you cutting small snippets of HTML code from their pages and pasting them onto yours. The resulting tools will actually be based on their computers, but look like they are on your web page. Remember, you won't please all your visitors all of the time, but good use of interactivity helps tip the scales in your favour.

Novice website designers seem drawn to hit counters like flies to meat. Avoid the temptation, they look awful and add no benefit to the users of your pages.

The form factor

An online form is no different to a paper form, other than that it appears on your computer screen and you don't need a stamp to post it. You will find them everywhere on the web, being used for such things as simple feedback through to ordering items from online shops or maybe asking for your email details so you can be informed of new developments. The common form factor is that they all require input from the user and result in an action from the website; in other words they add interactivity.

Anybody can create their own forms to include on their web pages; at their most basic they are only another collection of HTML tags, after all. However, things get a lot more complicated when it comes to creating the bit behind the scenes that processes the information entered into the form when the user hits the Submit button. This is where those 'scripts' that we mentioned on the last page come in, and where most ISPs leave the room. A CGI script, which stands for Common Gateway Interface in case you wondered, is a gateway between the web page and the computer upon which the web pages are actually stored and served up to the public. Most ISPs won't let you use your own scripts because they could pose a threat to their security, either through intent or just bad programming. Many web hosting companies will provide a range of approved scripts though, so it is worth checking with them to find out.

Forms the easy way

The easiest way to create a form is to let your web authoring software take the strain, as most will have a form menu bursting with options. Text entry is by way of either a one line box, or a larger box with scrollbars. There are three types of selection process, a checkbox or a 'radio' button (one is square with a tick in it, the other is round with a

blob in it) plus a drop-down menu list. And finally there is a Submit button that users press to send off the information when they are finished.

```
<form ACTION="mailto:davey@hap
pygeek.com" method="post">
<p align="left">
<br>
<br>
Your Name:<input type=text
name="name" size="50">
<br>
<br>
Your Email:<input type=text
NAME="email" size="50">
<br>
<br>
Comments:<TEXTAREA NAME="com
ments" rows="11" cols="43"
></textarea>
<br>
<br>
<input type="submit" value="Send
Now">
<br>
<br>
</p>
</form>
```

Under the surface it's just more HTML code, and not very much of it at that...

However, to the web page browser it's a functional and good looking form.

Reader Feedback

Your views are important to us, please complete this form to let us know what you think. We will not sell this information on to any third party.

Your Name:

Your Email:

Comments:

Send Now

You've got mail

Every website should include contact information, and one of the easiest ways to provide this is by way of email. After all, if someone is reading your website the chances are they have an email account and so it would be good if they could just click on a link and be able to dash off an email message there and then. As luck would have it, this is made possible by the use of a tiny snippet of HTML coding known as the 'mailto'.

The mailto link

If you really don't want to go to the bother of creating a simple form, then the mailto has to be the most convenient alternative, both from the point of view of the person using it and you getting it onto your web pages. Indeed, it is so simple to implement that you can discreetly tuck an email link at the bottom of every page on your website so as to remove the 'I can't be bothered to find it' argument from the feedback equation. A mailto is, when all is said and done, just another hyperlink but rather than whisking the person who clicks on it off to another web page, it automatically pops up either a form or the user's email software depending on which browser they are using, and what version of that browser. Internet Explorer 4, for example, requires the user to have Outlook Express installed for a mailto to work. The clever thing, though, is that when it does work it will already have your correct feedback email address already filled in; all the user has to do is type their message and hit Send. As always, web authoring software makes including a mailto link a simple matter of clicking on a button and entering the details of where the email should be sent and what text should appear on screen as the link itself. This link text is important, as we've already established that some people won't be able to make use of the mailto itself, so the text can spell out the email address anyway for them to cut and paste into their email software.

A mailto is a marvellous thing – click on one of these...

...and one of these pops up, with the recipient address already filled in!

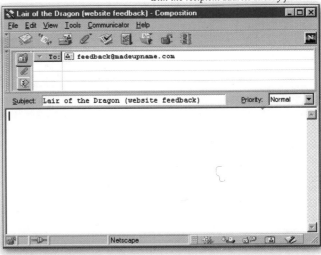

It's good to talk

Chat forums are the ultimate in interactivity when it comes to your website. They add value by turning your site into a community, and keep people coming back for more as a bonus. Providing such a feature may sound daunting to the novice website creator, but it doesn't have to be – especially if you leave all the hard work to someone else.

A chatroom of your own

There are numerous free chatroom services on the web that enable you to add web based chat facilities with the minimum of fuss and in less time than it takes to boil a kettle and make a cup of tea. You connect to the web page concerned, complete a few forms giving details of who you are and where your website is, and then it's just a matter of cutting and pasting the code that makes it all work from their web page into yours. There are step by step instructions all the way, and even if you have managed to avoid all contact with raw HTML by using web authoring software you needn't feel out of your depth. Most authoring software will let you see and edit the HTML by simply clicking on an 'HTML' tab or selecting an option from the menu, so you just open the relevant page, click on the HTML tab and paste the code straight in.

You don't install any new software on your computer, nor does the chatroom run from your web server (the computer that holds your web pages) so there are no problem's with getting permission from your ISP. Most of these chat facilities will work by connecting the user to the chat provider's website, and this is where all the work is actually done. However, the chatroom will look like it is running on your website, and most of your users will be none the wiser. The price you pay for these free services is that they can tend to run slowly when they are really busy, and usually they display banner adverts from sponsors.

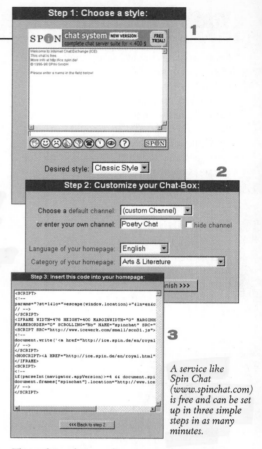

A service like Spin Chat (www.spinchat.com) is free and can be set up in three simple steps in as many minutes.

The result is a chatroom that appears to be on your web page, but is actually on the Spin Chat website.

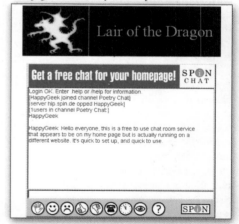

Adding a guest book to your website

There are many ways to add a guest book feature to your website, and before you do anything else you might want to call your ISP or web hosting company to see if they can provide you with this facility free of charge. However, if they don't or can't, then the simplest way of getting a book for your visitors to sign is to use a third party web-based service. There are plenty of free guest book services available, and they all work in much the same way but we are using the one at 4AllFree (www.4allfree.com) for the purposes of this example.

1 Connect to the free guest book service, and sign up. Be sure to check the terms of use and frequently asked questions (FAQ) section first though. Once you have joined up, which costs nothing, you can enter the website.

2 Once you've signed up and logged in as a member, you can check out some of the useful bits and pieces 4AllFree provides to help you enhance your own web-site. Scroll down the page until you see the 'Guest Book' entry and click on the 'Get Code' button which will take you to another page containing the necessary snippets of HTML code required to get things moving.

3 And here they are, three options: a straight-for-ward text link, a graphical link or a button to press. Whichever you choose, you just cut and paste it straight onto your web page in the same way as the chatroom example earlier.

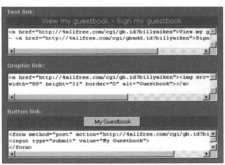

4 Here are all three options as they appear on our web page having just cut and pasted the code straight into our web authoring editor. Which you think looks best is a matter of personal taste, but we like the button so we shall use that.

Adding a guestbook (continued)

5 You can edit the text of the button by looking at the HTML code you have pasted, and changing the bit that says value="My Guestbook" and replacing "My Guestbook" with something else. The button will grow to accommodate your text, but brief is best we think.

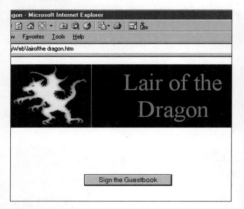

6 Click on the button and you will be taken to your guest book if everything has been cut and pasted properly so far. Then go back to the 4AllFree home page and hit the 'config' button in the guest book section so you can fine-tune things.

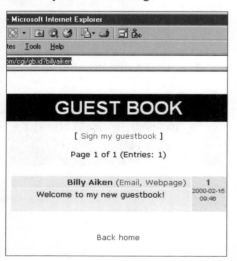

7 Here you can change the entry fields that appear in your guest book, decide what information your visitors have to enter (like their name and email address for example), change the general style of the book, block sexual comments, and even add an option that automatically sends each visitor a 'thank you for visiting' email.

8 Now when visitors click the guest book button they will be taken to your custom designed form, and slowly but surely your guest book archive of visitors' comments will build up.

CHAPTER 8 **Multimedia**

Web-based multimedia

So far we have looked at building an effective web presence using a combination of text, graphics, interactivity and good old fashioned common sense when it comes to design and layout. Now is the time to throw caution to the wind and have some fun by introducing some multimedia elements to your pages.

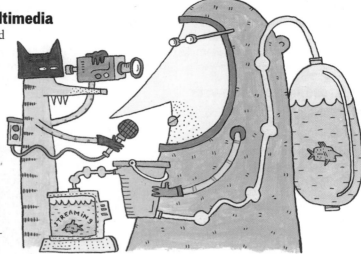

Imagination

Using your imagination and the vast array of tools that are available to help on the practical side of things, it is quite possible to greatly enhance the website experience for your visitors with the addition of just a little music or video. It is vital, however, that you keep your multimedia ambitions in perspective and balance what they add to the site very carefully with what they take away. What they add is an undoubted visual or audio impact, the 'wow factor' that makes your website stand out from the crowd. Unfortunately, every single page that finds itself graced by such additions also gains weight in terms of file size, which means it will take longer to download. The slickest bit of multimedia is no use to anyone if nobody hangs around for it to download before visiting the next website on their travels.

Know your limits

The trick to implementing web-based multimedia successfully is to know when enough is enough. Size does matter,

although the streaming techniques we'll discuss in a moment make it less important than it used to be. Your multimedia content should still be concise and relevant; there's no excuse for padding when someone else is paying to download it.

Multimedia content can bring a whole new aspect of the web into your browser. ITN (www.itn.co.uk) lets you watch the news as well as read it, for example.

ITN World News can be seen live 22:30 weekday evenings

Getting plugged in

Even though web browser software has come a long way in a short time, it is still too much to expect it to be able to deal with all the different multimedia formats that appear online.

Extending your browser

This is where plug-ins take centre stage. These small software programs extend the functionality of your web browser, seamlessly displaying video, or 3D walkthroughs, or playing music files. The most impressive plug-ins will integrate with your browser so the multimedia content plays right there in the same window as the web page, for all intents and purposes playing straight off the page itself. Some don't do this, and instead launch a separate window in which the movie is presented. A little careful positioning of this window can create much the same effect as full integration anyway.

Where to find what you need

There are literally hundreds of plug ins available and they range from the wildly popular such as Quicktime and RealPlayer, to the rather obscure that exist just to rotate 3D renditions of molecules for example. The web user will most likely not want to download a plug-in just to view content on your site, and your site alone. These are not trivial downloads, they are often 3Mb and upwards in size. So the savvy web designer will stick to making any multimedia content that is available on their pages in one of the more popular formats. This way the user is less likely to have to download and install new plug-ins, and so is more likely to hang around and look at your hard work. Even bearing this in mind, it is still a good idea to have a link on any pages that contain content requiring a plug-in to the download site for that software. That way if someone is without the software at least finding it is only a click or two away.

The most common multimedia plug-in formats to look out for include RealPlayer for both audio and video content, Quicktime for movies and Flash for animations (which we will look at in some depth in the next chapter). For more information on the vast range of plug-ins available, take a look at the Plug in Plaza website (http://browser-watch.internet.com/plug-in.html).

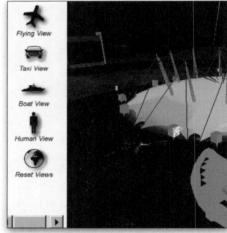

The Dome2000 website (www.dome2000.co.uk) features a 3D flyover of the Dome itself, but you'll need to download a 4Mb plug-in to be able to see it.

RealPlayer doesn't work inside the web browser, but does come with its own television-like control console to give you full control over audio and video content.

Streaming not screaming

Most plug-ins manage to speed up the process of actually hearing the music or watching the video. Until fairly recently most achieved this by use of a technique called compression, where the file itself was squashed up so it was smaller to download, and then the plug-in would inflate it again on your computer and play it when it was back to normal. But there is only so much squashing even the best plug-in can manage, and so website designers had to keep the multimedia clip itself as small as possible to start with. The user still had to download the whole thing and wait for it to be decompressed before playing it as well.

Video for Real

A technique called streaming has recently surfaced and taken the web world by storm. Any plug-in that uses streaming, RealPlayer for example, lets the user start watching the movie or listening to the music almost immediately. At most there will only be a delay of a few seconds before your multimedia web page comes to life. Streaming works by downloading the file into a storage area on your computer which acts like a small bucket. The video or audio information fills the bucket up very quickly because of its small size and as soon as it starts pouring out over the top the movie can start playing. All the time the bucket itself continues to be kept

full whilst the file downloads and a constant stream of information pours out and onto your screen. RealPlayer take connect speeds into account and adjusts the rate at which they let information flow out of the storage buffer accordingly, thus ensuring the movie is smooth and not choppy.

Apart from speeding up the whole multimedia experience online, streaming also lets users switch off the video after a few seconds if they don't like it, and this saves them from having to download the whole file before discovering it's not for them. Streaming also means that you can put larger multimedia files on your website because the overall download time is no longer such a big issue.

One of the great things to come from streaming technology is the ability to transmit live broadcasts from around the world. Unfortunately, live streaming is beyond the scope of amateur website builders.

Video on demand

Moving pictures have opened up a new dimension to the web page, allowing you to let others truly experience 'being there' no matter where in the world they actually are. Digital camcorders are commonplace nowadays, and so getting film into your computer is a lot easier and less expensive than it used to be. If you haven't got access to a digital camcorder, though, you will still have to spend some money to get hold of the necessary digitiser card to slot into your PC to be able to capture moving image from tape. A cheaper, and certainly very popular, compromise between the two is to use a low cost and readily available webcam instead. These devices simply plug into your PC and sit on top of the monitor. They are cheap, small, and perfect for capturing video clips to put on your web page.

Streaming from home

To get the file from your computer and onto the web page is also pretty straightforward, and doesn't have to cost anything either. If you use software like the free version of the RealProducer program (downloadable from http://www.real.com) you can make the resulting video very user-friendly indeed. This is because RealProducer will compress the video file to make it physically smaller to start with, plus it then optimises the file for the type of connection speed expected from your visitors. It's best to play it safe and go for something basic such as the 28.8k modem speed, that way you keep everyone happy. This process can dramatically reduce the overall size of your video clip; a 20Mb video can easily come down to around 500k. Because streaming is also used, the file size is perfectly acceptable and won't spoil anyone's fun. You should check with your ISP or web hosting company that they support streaming, either in software or hardware, to be on the safe side though. Alternatives to RealPlayer include the ever

popular Quicktime which also provides streaming support, and the non-streaming but very popular MPEG format. MPEG files tend to be on the larger side, and they have to be downloaded in their entirety before they can be played on your computer. On the plus side though, there are numerous free players available.

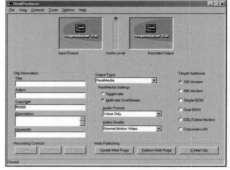

RealProducer comes in a free version that lets you control all the important aspects of getting your video onto the web, making it smaller and faster.

You can see what's happening in an internet café in Latvia (www.binet.lv/cafe/camera.hts), with a new video clip uploaded every five minutes, thanks to the wonder of the webcam.

Sound advice

When done properly the addition of sound to your website can make a world of difference, setting the mood or providing a commentary to accompany the text on screen. If done badly there is nothing that will make people head for the 'stop' button and move on to the next site on their list quite as quickly. So what do we mean by badly, exactly? Well, it's never a good idea to force people to listen to your taste in music without them having any choice in the matter. Whilst you can make music play in the background it is bad manners not to provide some method of turning it off because the user may not like it. This isn't difficult to implement in Internet Explorer, as you'll see in our step by step guide to getting music on your page.

The long arm of the law

Beware of copyright issues surrounding the use of music online, or you could find yourself in trouble. If you want to make use of a particular piece of music then you must seek the permission of whoever owns the copyright before going ahead and doing it. Alternatively use copyright free music or record your own original track.

Keeping it small

Watch your file sizes; a standard WAV format audio file of three minutes of music may easily be 25Mb, whereas the same track in the much talked about MP3 format would be just 2Mb. The MP3 file would also have the advantage of being much better quality and can be streamed using the RealPlayer plug-in so it starts playing before the file is fully downloaded. You can use the RealPlayer plug-in that also plays video content for playing MP3 files, which is why they are now the Internet's music standard. But that only applies if you are making music available for download from your site. If, however, you just want background

music then you are still best off using good old fashioned MIDI files, which are extremely small (10K for 30 seconds worth) so download quickly, which is important if the music is meant to be an integral part of the page design.

Try MP3.com (www.mp3.com) for a truly staggering choice of online music. It's also a good place to go to learn more about the MP3 format.

If it's sound effects rather than music you want, then try WavCentral (www.wavcentral.com).

Adding sound to your web page

The simplest way of adding sound to your website is by inserting a little piece of HTML code that instructs a web browser to download and play an audio file. Unfortunately, the two main browsers work in different ways with sound, so the results will vary. Do bear in mind our advice about copyright issues and file sizes though; if you are in any doubt about the legality of the first or the enormity of the second then your best bet is to leave your pages silent!

1 If you don't already have a piece of music to use then look for copyright free MIDI files at one of the big search engines, and you'll be presented with plenty of choice. Better still, ask around and see if anyone can produce a piece of music just for your site – if you have musical friends this is certainly the best approach.

2 Sometimes the spoken word can have a lot of impact. If you wanted a short personalised voice greeting for your home page, then you can record this yourself using the sound recorder built into Windows (it's located in the Accessories folder) and save it as a WAV file. Windows Recorder comes with some simple special effects too.

3 Microsoft's FrontPage lets you incorporate background sound into your web pages. But, watch out – only Internet Explorer supports this <bgsound> HTML tag and there is no easy way of getting any control panel to pop up on the page. For this reason, it's best avoided in this instance.

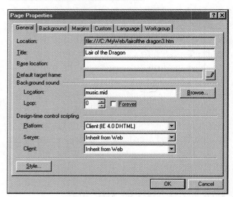

4 Instead you should either go straight to the HTML window of your web authoring software, or be brave and experiment with entering the HTML code straight into Windows Notepad, saving as an HTML file. The code shown will play the background sound in Internet Explorer only.

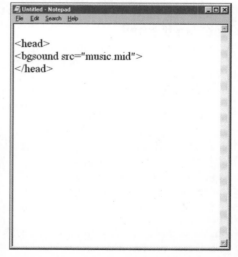

5 Using the <embed> tag as shown is much better than the <bgsound> we used before. It works in both Internet Explorer and Netscape, and it lets us do some pretty clever little tricks.

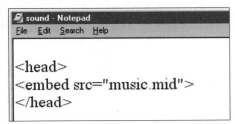

6 By cutting and pasting that same little bit of text into the HTML of our example 'Lair of the Dragon' page, when we look at it in Netscape Navigator a small control panel appears that lets the user choose to play, pause or stop the music.

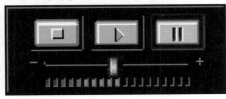

7 Exactly the same cut and pasted snippet produces a slightly less flashy but none the less functional result in Internet Explorer. You can play around with the size variables and screen positioning until you are happy with it.

8 Alternatively you could just drop a hyperlink such as the following:

```
<a href="music.mid">Listen to this!</a>
```

anywhere on your page which, when clicked, pops up a control panel window in Netscape or this Windows media player in Internet Explorer.

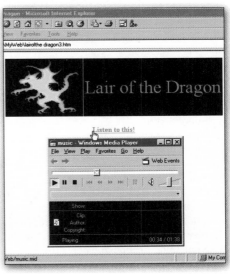

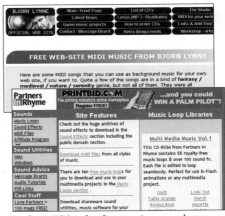

For free MIDI and audio to use in your web pages, check out sites such as www.lynnemusic.com and www.partnersinrhyme.com

CHAPTER 9 Getting animated

Web-based animation

When we say animation we don't mean to suggest that you should turn your web pages into your own version of the Cartoon Network. Instead, the kind of animation we mean is more along the dictionary definition of 'vivacity, bringing something alive'. This sums up what you should aim to achieve using animation techniques; you want to add some jazz to your pages, make the content leap off the page and into the attention of your visitors.

Animation can take many forms, from the simplest of things such as icons that change from one thing to another when a user moves the mouse cursor over them, or logos that spin around for no apparent reason. Most banner adverts you see on web pages are not static, they do something to catch your attention, another example of using animation on the page. Then there are the more advanced techniques such as the use of Java to run little programs inside your web browser window so as to provide a clock or pop up a message window when the user clicks on part of the screen for example. The most obviously animated websites are those that use Macromedia Shockwave, a multimedia presentation package that changes the web page into something more akin to a TV screen, complete with lots of action and interactivity. As you might imagine, there are lots of do's and don'ts to be absorbed to ensure you make a

splash and not a mess of your pages. Read on for some sage advice...

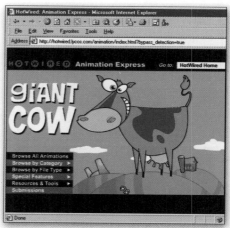

Animation Express (http://hotwired.lycos.com/animation) is a superb showcase of what can be achieved by animating your pages. But your attempts can be a lot more subtle than this 'in your face' approach.

Do's and don'ts of animated interactivity

Beyond the obvious advice of don't overdo it – you want to highlight aspects of your page and its contents not hide them with lots of whoosh and whizzbang – there are plenty of specific hints and tips that even some experienced web designers could do well to remember. It seems that in their desire to impress their clients with their cleverness, some website designers forget the basic principles of simplicity and content above all. If you want to include an animated logo, and there is no reason why you shouldn't despite what those amusing IBM television adverts have to say about the matter, then make sure you give it a transparent background as described in Chapter 6. This will ensure that the animation becomes part of the page, and not apart from it. The appearance you are aiming for is 'floating, not gloating' – write that down on a post-it note and stick it on your monitor; it is very valuable advice indeed.

Keep it lean

If you are tempted by the lure of Java, then wake up and smell the coffee before getting carried away. Although there are plenty of free small 'applets', Java programs that appear to run from within your web page, they can cost the visitor dear if overdone. Each applet has first to be downloaded to the visitor's PC, and then run just like any other program. Well, almost, because they are running inside the browser they can eat away at your system's memory resources. Put too many on a single page and you can slow down the browsing process to a crawl, and even crash your visitor's computer in extreme cases. The size argument also applies to the use of Shockwave to create those multimedia CD-like experiences favoured by many big websites. Despite advances in technology, Shockwave pages are still on the large side, as is the Shockwave flash plug-in required to view

them. Always provide a clearly marked entry path to your website, one for Shockwave users and one for everyone else. Otherwise people on dial-up modem connections may get fed up with staring at the 'Made with Macromedia' logo and go elsewhere.

Developers use lots of tricks, like the 'let's play a game' ruse to divert your attention from the fact that the content is taking an age to download!

Sites such as Gamelan (www.gamelan.com) have hundreds of interesting Java applets to download, but don't be tempted to overdo it.

Animated GIFs

In Chapter 6 we explained all about GIFs, image files ideal for website use as logos thanks to their small size and limited 256 colour support. GIFs are also ideal for animating, and have become the de facto standard for adding eye-catching but often annoying on screen action to the web page. Which is not to say that these things are pointless; if they do their job and get the attention of someone who otherwise may have clicked on past your pages they have served a useful purpose. Nowhere can this be demonstrated more effectively than in their most popular application, the advertising banner. If you've seen a small advert at the top of a web page that appears to spin around, or has new information sliding into view every few seconds, then the chances are you have experienced an animated GIF doing its job.

A sequence of images

The animated GIF file is actually downloaded by a visiting web browser in the same way as any other graphic image on the page; indeed it even looks the same on the outside because it masquerades as a single GIF format file. However, in actual fact the GIF file itself is more like an envelope, inside which you will find a series of frames that make up the final picture. When the web browser encounters these images it displays them one by one, in turn, until it reaches the end when it will stop or loop the whole process again. This gives the appearance of animation without the need for any special plug-ins or additional software; all that's needed to view it is an ordinary web browser.

What's more, expensive software isn't needed to create them either. Just about any graphics software program will let you make animated GIFs, plus there are shareware applications dedicated to this single task. If that wasn't enough, other folk who have

been there and done that already have whole website archives packed full of ready-made animated GIFs for you to download and include on your own pages, and most often these are yours to use at no cost.

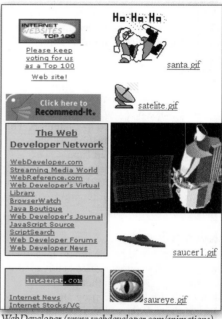

WebDeveloper (www.webdeveloper.com/animations) has a huge range of ready-made animated GIFs, free of charge for non-commercial use. You can see them all in action before downloading them.

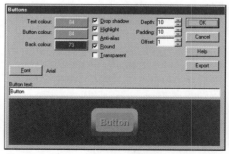

Or you could use a dedicated application such as the Gif Construction Set to create animated buttons etc (www.mindworkshop.com/alchemy/gifconcl.html).

Getting flashy

Animated GIFs are great for creating small, fast, eye-catching blasts of action on your page, but they are not really suited for anything more adventurous. If you want to move up a notch in terms of what you can do, then you will need to use Macromedia Flash or Shockwave. These tools enable animated presentations that are so smooth and professional, in the right hands of course, that they are even used to create the Comedy Central TV cartoon series, *South Park*. It is worth stressing though, that these are not really something for the novice web designer to start messing about with. Whilst the browser plug-ins that enable people to view both Flash and Shockwave enhanced pages is free of charge, the applications that let web designers create the content in the first place most certainly are not.

Shockwave and Flash

Shockwave content is created using Macromedia Director, whereas Flash content is created with, well, Flash. Although often confused, the two are very different beasts. Flash is used to create interactive web pages featuring those high impact graphics, animations and sound. Shockwave content is more geared towards multimedia demos, games and such like. With Shockwave the multimedia is 'off the page' and is confined to the player window, whereas Flash is windowless and fully integrated as part of the page itself. Think of Shockwave as creating movies for your web page (many CD-based games are put together using Director), and Flash creating a user experience and you won't be far off the mark. Of the two, Flash would seem to be the more suited to web page design. It is seamless, uses streaming so it is instant, manages to compress files to a fairly small size and can do some neat tricks like allowing the user to zoom in on content. It also has the advantage over Shockwave of being

easier to learn from the novice web designer's point of view. Luckily there is an evaluation version available that you can download so you can try before you buy – for 30 days at any rate.

Visit Shockwave.com (www.shockwave.com) for a showcase of exactly what is possible using this technology. When you get there you will see that this whole page is alive!

You can find out more about Flash at the Macromedia website (www.macromedia.co.uk) where you can also download an evaluation version to play with.

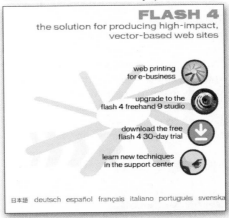

The Java jive

Java is a programming language with a difference: it doesn't care what computer platform it is running on. This independence makes it ideally suited for the web, which also doesn't care what computers people are using to look at web pages. Programs written in Java are called 'applets' which is apt, because they are like mini versions of bigger applications. When a web browser connects to a page with a Java applet featured, it downloads this small applet and runs it locally on that person's computer. However, the applet appears within the browser, for all intents and purposes as if it is running directly on the web page. It is a good illusion, and one that many web designers have hurried to include on their pages. Then there is JavaScript, which does much the same thing as Java but, instead of requiring an applet to be downloaded and run, performs its magic straight from the web page. JavaScript works by the use of what can most easily be described as an extension to HTML. The JavaScript code snippet is simply cut and pasted straight into your HTML code between ‹script› tags.

Java or JavaScript?

There are two main differences between Java and JavaScript. First, Java will work straight out of the box, as it were, as both Internet Explorer and Netscape have support built in to the browser. JavaScript, however, was developed originally by Netscape and just like ordinary HTML code can require tweaking to get it to work properly in the Microsoft browser as well. The second difference is to do with usage. Java applets tend to be things that provide a service such as a currency converter or mini spreadsheet, for example, whilst JavaScript is more often used for surface gloss like making something on screen change into something else when the mouse moves over them (known as a rollover).

So which should you use? To be honest it doesn't really matter as long as you use them sparingly. Both ready-made Java applets and snippets of JavaScript code are readily available on the web from specialist archives. Just download what you need, insert it into your web page and it's done with.

The JavaScript Source (http://javascript.internet.com) has hundreds of ready-made code scripts for you to download and insert into your HTML free of charge.

See Java in action at NetCharts (www.netcharts.com).

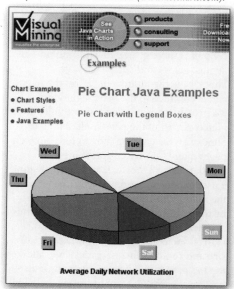

Creating your own animated banner

Probably the most popular use of the animated GIF is for making an eye-catching banner advert. Even though they can look very complicated, it is quite easy to create a simple and effective animated banner in less than 10 minutes. We have chosen to use the 'Animation Shop' software that is bundled along with Paint Shop Pro, because it is very easy to use, yet produces excellent results. Paint Shop Pro is one of the cheaper graphics programs on the market, yet its powerful tools make it a popular choice for those entering web design for the first time.

1 Load up Animation Shop, go to the File menu and select 'Banner Wizard' to get things started. This automates the process of creating a fully animated banner that looks as if it was lovingly crafted by a skilled professional.

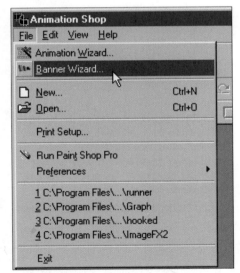

2 The first window from the wizard lets you select either a transparent background or a colour of your own choice. Transparent backgrounds will make the animation appear to float on the page, which is what we want in this case. Clicking the opaque button lets you choose a colour from a pop-up palette.

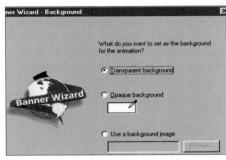

3 Next you can choose the size of your banner from a range of well described options, or specify your own size. We've gone for a half size banner.

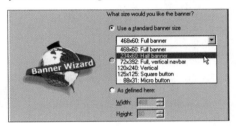

4 You can leave the length and frame rate at the default values for now; you can always play with them later to get the exact result you want. The only other choice here is to opt for looping or not. If you loop the animation it will just continue playing, providing the web browser supports that function.

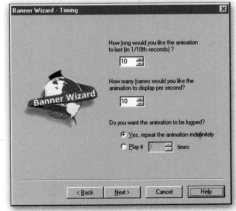

Creating an animated banner (continued)

5 Enter the text you want to display in your banner, and then use the Font button to change the font and size. Because your banner will be a graphic you don't have to worry about using a font that the viewer may not have, so be creative. You can choose the text colour from the next screen.

6 And now the fun begins. Select a transition effect, and your banner will be rendered and previewed. If the text is too large or too small, then you can use the back button to change it until you are happy. The Customise button lets you change things like the speed of movement or angle of bounce for the effects that you have applied.

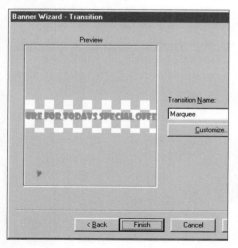

7 You now have an animated GIF banner ready to use on your web page. Just save the file, choosing between best image quality or smaller file size. The image will be optimised, and this handy report shows how small the file is and how quickly it will download. Then it's just a matter of copying the GIF file to your web folder and inserting it onto the page as you would any other image, make it a hyperlink, and you are done.

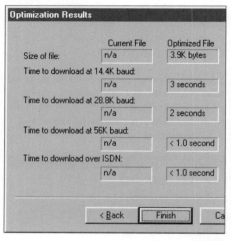

8 You'll have to take our word for it that the text is scrolling across the page inside a transparent box – that's why you can't see that it actually reads "Click here for today's special offer!" It is eye-catching, just begging the visitor to click on it, yet took less than 10 minutes to create.

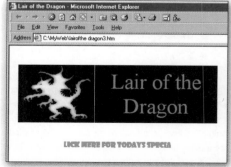

CHAPTER 10

Making your website pay

Money, Money, Money

There is money to be made from the web, of that there is little doubt. You've only got to read the financial pages of any newspaper and you'll see the stories of ordinary people whose web-based businesses are worth millions of pounds. Every successful web business has to start somewhere. The Yahoo! search directory started life as a collection of links to the pages visited by two students, compiled in their bedroom on campus. Or closer to home there's the 17-year-old schoolboy, Benjamin Cohen, who set up a website called JewishNet on a budget of just £150. The site became so successful that within a year financial backers had invested in it, changed the name to SoJewish.com

and put a value of £5 million on the business. The great thing about the web is that there is nothing stopping anyone with a good idea and a lot of luck from joining the ranks of the internet millionaires, but the odds are stacked against it actually happening for you. For every website that does strike gold, there are hundreds of thousands that don't. There is no such thing as a guaranteed money-maker online, and there is no easy route to riches. So the first thing you have to ask is do you really want to make money from your website, or are you happy with it being a 'for pleasure and not profit' exercise? If the answer is a resounding yes on the financial front, then read on and we'll explain some of the options available to you.

SoJewish.com

The UK's first and leading Web site for the Jewish community plans to capitalise on its market lead - and is set to turn a schoolboy into a multi-millionaire before he sits his A levels! JewishNet.co.uk was set up by Benjamin Cohen, 17, ten months ago with just £150, and is already valued at over £5million.

With the support of investment and securities group, Durlacher, Epoch Software has brokered a deal with IDesk together with the London Jewish News to back Benjamin's site, which will be completely relaunched in February 2000, and is expected to float on the stock market in April/May 2000. The site moves from it's current address at JewishNet.co.uk to a new home at SoJewish.com later this year.

Benjamin Cohen, the Creator of JewishNet.co.uk
e-mail him at ben@cyberbritain.co.uk
or chat to him online with AOL Instant Messenger screen name CYBERBRITAIN

Benjamin Cohen, a 17-year-old student, created the JewishNet site a year ago — now it's being rebranded as SoJewish.com and is valued at £5 million.

Advertising

When most people think about ways of making money from a website, the first thing that springs to mind is advertising. After all, just about every big website you visit will have advert banners on display. Indeed, advertising is ideally suited to the web page. Unlike all other forms of advertising which require the potential customer to get up and make an effort to visit a shop, make a phone call or whatever, web adverts just involve a single click and the customer is whisked off to the shop. Whilst online advertising is undoubtedly big business, raking in hundreds of millions of pounds each year across the board, the vast majority of the money goes to a small percentage of the biggest sites. The reason for this is simple: the people paying for advertising generally do so based on either on the number of people seeing the advert on the page, or the number of people clicking on the advert and arriving at the shop. In either case, the rates paid are often low, just a few pounds per thousand viewers or clicks, so only those websites pulling in millions of people every month stand any real chance of making any significant amount of money this way.

Selling space

With most banner advertising being handled by specialist advertising agencies, the chances are that your small website wouldn't even make it onto their books. Which is not to say that you can't take the DIY approach, and sell targeted advertising space yourself. If your website is about your town or village, then approach local businesses and see if they would be interested; if it's about fish-

ing then approach businesses in that industry, and so on. The key to success here is to make the offer an attractive one, which means keeping the rates low. You should also expect to be able to show potential advertisers how busy your website is, by producing statistics from your ISP or web hosting company showing the number of visitors or 'hits' you get on a monthly basis. Therefore, it is best to wait a while until your website has attracted a regular audience of sufficient numbers to appeal to the paying advertiser.

Freeserve (www.freeserve.net) has tremendous pulling power and attracts a lot of advertising money based on millions of visitors every week. You can't expect to do the same with your website, no matter how good it is.

Web-based advertising agencies like DoubleClick (www.doubleclick.com) will generally only take on the bigger websites.

Setting up shop

It is possible to make money by advertising someone else's business from your website, but it is likely to be small change at best. The obvious alternative is to start your own web-based business. The web is the perfect place to set up shop: it is open 365 days a year, 24 hours a day, and your customers could come from anywhere in the world.

Fridges to Inuits

You need something to sell of course; an empty shop is an empty shop online or off. If you have a hobby knitting baby clothes, making chocolates or painting pictures, for example, then there is no reason why you shouldn't be able to showcase these talents on the web and sell to interested browsers. Or you could sell services instead – how about a course teaching others how to knit, bake or paint?

It's in the bag

Setting up shop can be as simple as a website showcasing these products, taking orders by telephone or email and accepting payments by cheque in the post, or as complex as a store with shopping basket facilities allowing items to be added at the click of a button, and accepting payments by credit card using secure facilities. Which you choose depends on how serious you are and how much money you have to spend. If you just want to test the water then keep it simple; but if you want to launch an online business then you should invest in business strength tools.

There is a third option, which sits between advertising another shop and starting your own, namely the affiliate scheme. These work on a commission basis, much like Christmas hamper sales or mail order fashion catalogues. You advertise the service on your site; in the case of book sales you may have a search box allowing people to hunt down the book they want, or maybe just a simple 'buy books here' logo. In either case, when someone goes to buy a book they actually do so at Amazon, but you get a percentage of that sale by way of commission.

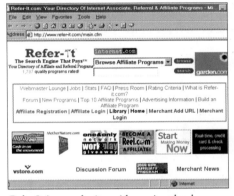

Refer-It (www.refer-it.com) has reviewed and rated more than 1500 affiliate schemes, and provides the perfect place to explore this particular money-making avenue.

Actinic Catalogue (www.actinic.co.uk) is one of the most popular ways to build a professional online shop for a modest investment.

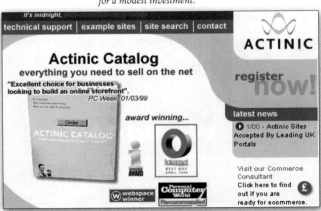

Show me the money

Imagine a shop without a till, where the shop assistant couldn't take a cheque or a credit card but insisted upon cash. If you think about it there aren't many shops like that in the high street, because they couldn't compete with all the other shops that make paying for goods as easy as possible. So it is on the web, and although you can set up shop and only take payment by way of a cheque in the post, these kind of businesses are viewed as 'hobby' shops rather than serious, and can lose trade as a result. Which all makes sense, but if you are not already an existing high street shopkeeper how can you go about accepting credit card payments on the web?

Cutting in the middle man

The answer is that you pay a third party to deal with the payments for you, and these are called Payment Service Providers or PSPs for short. When someone gets to the checkout of your web shop they have to fill in their payment details, and pressing the Buy Now button sends that form securely to the PCP computer for processing. They check that the card details are genuine, authorise the sale and deduct the money from the credit card. Of course, this comes at a price to you; usually there will be a monthly fee plus a percentage taken from every sale. An alternative could be the use of electronic cash. Customers register with a currency provider such as eCash (http://www.ecashtechnologies.com), open an account and buy some eCash using their credit card. Web shops accepting eCash take this as payment and redeem it for real cash. These kind of web-based currencies are in their infancy, but worth keeping an eye on, not least because they bring the opportunity to charge very small amounts for goods, known as micropayments, that are not viable using credit cards. You can't go into a newsagent and buy a packet of polos with a credit card because it would cost more to process the transaction than the value of the sale. Using a micropayment system though, you could charge 1/10th of a penny to view a web page, if you so wished.

Alternative currencies such as eCash (www.ecashtechnologies.com) could be something to consider, especially if you only want to charge very small amounts for services offered.

WorldPay (www.worldpay.com) is one of the best known Payment Service Providers, offering an easy way to accept credit card payments from your website.

Practicalities and problems

Whenever you start thinking in terms of making money from your website then the issue of keeping on the right side of the law must figure strongly in your thoughts at all times. Just because you are doing business on the internet doesn't mean that you can get away with skirting around the law; in fact there are more potential pitfalls to watch out for than if you were trading in the high street. The obvious legal guidelines apply, such as not misleading customers with inaccurate descriptions of items for sale, having to live up to your side of the bargain and supply the goods for which you take payment, and to clearly indicate costs including any delivery charges. Which brings us straight on to possible pitfall number one, delivering goods to a global market. Remember that the web is global, and your customers could come from anywhere around the world. Unless you specifically state that you can only supply goods within the UK, make sure you show clearly how much it will cost to deliver items to Europe and the rest of the world. Otherwise you could find yourself having to bear the additional delivery costs yourself.

No getting away from tax

Another area which it would be nice to think didn't apply to the web, but unfortunately does, is the small matter of taxable income. If you are selling goods from your website then you must declare this on your income tax return and pay any taxes due on your profits. The same applies to revenue from advertising on your pages, naturally. Whilst on the subject of advertising, there are some practical hints which you should take into account to get the best results for your sponsors. The standard size of a banner is 468 × 60 pixels, and it is usually located within the top 400 pixels of a web page. This is because these have proven to be the best size and position to attract the

eye. Adding the words 'click here' to a banner advert actually does work, and animated banners perform much better than static ones. See Chapter 9 for a guide to animating a banner.

Clearly stated postage costs and estimated delivery times are essential to your site. Take a look at Amazon (www.amazon.co.uk) for a good example of clearly explained policies.

The Internet Advertising Bureau (www.iab.net) has a useful guide to standard advertising banner sizes.

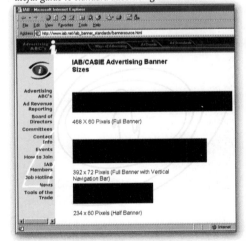

Resources for would-be web millionaires

The web itself is packed with resources of help to anyone wanting to find out more about turning an ordinary website into a moneyspinner. Unfortunately, if you do a search for 'money-making' or similar at any of the big search engine sites you will get drowned in pages offering get rich quick schemes, online share trading and all sorts of other things. So to help cut to the chase, here is our quick guide to some of the most helpful websites to check out first.

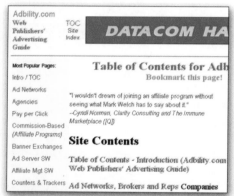

Adbility (www.adbility.com) is a good starting point to learn all you need to know about the business of advertising on the web. The site has advice and guidance for webmasters, and reviews of all the major agencies and services available.

The Income Café (www.theincomecafe.com) is a one-stop shop with links to all sorts of pages that can help generate an income for your website. There is a particularly complete listing of affiliate programs of all kinds.

Yahoo Stores (http://store.yahoo.com) provides an easy way into setting up a high profile web shop with only a few items for sale. It's free for 10 days so you can get it going, but if you want to take orders you'll need to subscribe.

Abracadabra has an excellent overview of electronic cash and alternative web-based currencies, plus a good set of links to related sites (http://abracad.users.netlink.co.uk/emoney.html).

Become an Amazon Associate - step by step

Adding value to your pages by association is easy when you sign up with an affiliate scheme such as Amazon's, and you stand to earn a percentage of all sales made to people shopping through your site link. Becoming an Amazon Associate is easier than you may think – we will show you how in just four easy steps.

1 First go to the Amazon UK website and follow the 'Associates' link about two-thirds of the way down the page. After reading all the related information, click on the 'join now' button to proceed.

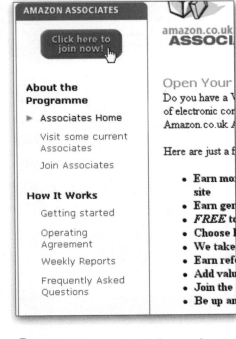

2 Next fill in the form that tells Amazon who you are, what your website is called and where it is located, and importantly where to send the cheque for that money you will (hopefully) make as a successful affiliate! Amazon will contact you by email to approve your application and provide the detailed instructions for adding the necessary links to your web page.

3 You can choose to link straight to the Amazon site via a logo of your choosing, or have a search box on your page to let users find the book they want. These two options offer 5% commission on all sales. Or you can link to specific books, with commission ranging from 5% to 15%. All options are achieved simply by cutting and pasting the HTML code as instructed in your approval email.

4 And the final result will look something like this, a link on your page that could earn you some useful pocket money. All you have to do now is get people clicking on it, which involves getting people into your site in numbers, which is what we will look at in the next chapter.

CHAPTER 11

Getting noticed

Website promotion

Once you have created your site and published the pages onto the web, it is tempting
to sit back and think that the visitors will
now come knocking at the door in droves.
Unfortunately it doesn't happen like that in
real life; no matter how good your website
actually is, if nobody knows it exists then
nobody is going to come and see it. Yes,
there is some truth in the fact that if you
leave it long enough then the various search
engine spiders (automated software programs that wander around the web looking
for new pages to add to the search site database) will find you. Yes, this does mean that
you will eventually get listed on various
search engine databases. And yes, it does
mean that your page about your love of
football will appear when someone searches
for that subject. What it doesn't mean is that
your website will appear at the top of the
listing of sites that meet the search criteria,
or in the top 50 sites, or top 1000 even. If
your website is lost towards the middle, or
worse, of a list of 10,000 sites then it's as
good as not being listed at all because people just don't bother digging down that far.

Make it easy to find

If you want people to come to your website
in volume, you've got to do some of the hard
marketing work yourself. Which means
designing a search-friendly site, informing
the search engines that you exist rather than
letting them find you, making use of all the
resources the internet provides.

*A simple search on 'football' returned nearly 8 million
matching results – if your website is listed below the
first 100 or so you probably won't get spotted. If it's at
1 million you can forget it altogether!*

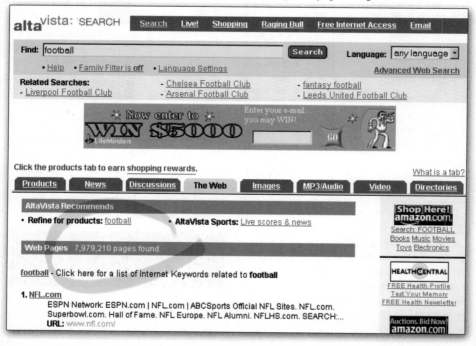

Search-friendly site design

As we've already explained, search sites use automated programs to collect information about web pages that then gets entered into the database at the heart of their particular search engine. Known as spiders (because they crawl around the web) or bots (a shortening of robot) these impersonal, invisible workers are your key to getting a good search engine listing. You need to design your website with them in mind, making sure that they can see all of your pages for a start, and that once they've been spotted the right kind of information is harvested. There are two types of search site, the directory and the engine. AltaVista (http://www.av.com) is an engine whilst Yahoo! (http://www.yahoo.co.uk) is a directory. Engines usually use the spider system to get information, although you can jump-start the process by submitting your website address to the site in question. Directories are commonly compiled by hand; you fill in a form about your site and then a real human being goes and reviews it before adding it the directory (or not, depending on what they find).

Catching spiders

Catering for search spiders means thinking carefully about some of your design and content, and a by-product of this is that the same principles generally benefit your human visitors as well. Things like having a title that is both informative and keyword heavy are important. This is because the first place a search spider looks is between the ‹title› tags in your HTML code. The search engine will also use this as the title of your page entry in their database, so it has to make sense to the human eye. You want to include as many relevant keywords as possible here, without turning the title into nonsense. So for a page about knitting cardigans, for example, a good title would be 'The wool cardigan knitting pattern craft page' because this includes the keywords 'cardigan, craft, knitting, pattern, wool' all of which are relevant to your site, without turning the title into nonsense. If you can use the same keywords or phrases in the body text of the page, all the better, because many search spiders look there as well.

AltaVista is a search engine, and uses software robots known as 'spiders' to hunt down new pages and add them automatically to the index.

Yahoo is a search directory, and uses real people to review new websites and add pages to its index.

Search-friendly site design (continued)

Some search engines will look for things called 'META' tags in the page code, although, because of misuse some sites don't bother with these at all any more. It does no harm to include them though, and your web authoring software should be able to help. If not, use one of the online resources such as the META tag generator (http://www.websitepromote.com/resources /meta) which will produce the code to cut and paste into your pages for free. META tags are simply HTML code containing descriptive keywords purely for the benefit of web search spiders to aid the indexing of your site. If your site uses frames, then make sure you use the 'noframes' option as described in Chapter 5. This way the search spider can see what is contained in the various frames, whereas without it they would only see the frameset content which means little to anything other than web browser software. Similarly, spiders don't see images, so make sure all images have a descriptive text attached using the 'ALT' function. Again, your web authoring software will let you add this to the code behind an image, and it is also useful to those people looking at your site with images turned off in their web browser to speed up loading of pages.

Follow the form

You should also bear some additional things in mind when going for a good listing at a search directory site such as Yahoo. Because they rely on users filling in a form to alert them to the existence of a new page or site in the first place, it is important that you fill this in strictly following their guidelines. So keep your descriptions accurate, don't try and get it listed in inappropriate categories, and above all else be brief with everything from page title to page description. You can help yourself to catch the reviewer's eye by making a good site to start with; a single page site that is very slow to load and once

loaded looks a mess stands a lower chance of getting listed than another which has multiple pages of consistently high quality and content.

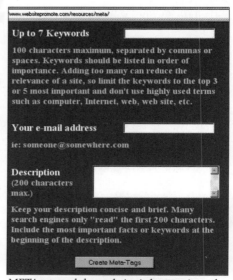

META tags can help search sites index your site, and free tools like this tag generator make adding them child's play.

Follow the instructions to the letter in order to give your site the smoothest ride through the Yahoo submission process – don't expect it to be quick, though, as submissions can take months to get listed.

Active marketing

Beyond getting listed on search sites, to get the maximum exposure, you need to put in a little effort proactively marketing your website online. Participate in relevant Usenet newsgroups, those discussion areas of the internet that cover every conceivable subject matter. Locate the groups that are linked to your interests and get chatting. Don't advertise blatantly, but offer advice when you can and always include your website address in your message signature. Talking of which, add that address to your email signature as well, and to 'real world' things such as letterheads and business cards.

You scratch mine

Reciprocal links are a tried and tested method of spreading the word about your site; you simply find another website on a similar subject and ask if they would add a link to your pages in return for you linking to theirs. This 'you scratch my back' system works very well, even amongst sites that you might imagine would be competing with each other. Web rings (http://www.webring.com) offer a similar resource, but you link to other similar websites in a more formal manner, complete with navigation tools that help the user jump between web ring member sites. This way people with that specific interest are more likely to find you. Anything that helps build a community of users is going to be a good thing, so implement some of the inter-active elements discussed in Chapter 7, such as a chatroom or guest book to encourage participation when users do find you.

Don't spread junk

One thing that you must not do, under any circumstances, is give in to the temptation to send junk mail to other internet users with information about your website. Whilst it is relatively easy to send the same advert to

thousands of Usenet newsgroups, or carbon copy the same message to everyone in your email address book, it is widely frowned upon. Let's be honest, do you appreciate any of the junk mail, also known as spam, that arrives in your mailbox? Apart from generating bad feeling, which is hardly the way to encourage people to visit your pages, spam doesn't work anyway as most people simply delete it on arrival without reading it.

Even the most unusual of subjects can find a web ring to help mutually promote their sites – like the Chihuahua Web Ring (www.iolinc.net/mlake/cring.htm).

The Coalition Against Unsolicited Commercial Email (www.cauce.com) will explain why you shouldn't use junk email in your online marketing campaign.

Using a search site submission wizard

There are a lot of search engine submission tools available, and most do pretty much the same thing in pretty much the same way. We have chosen the Exploit Wizard because it is one of the better known and very easy to use. It comes in two versions, the free edition that we are using for this example which submits your website details to 20 different search engines, and a registered edition which costs £20 for a month's usage but lets you automatically submit your details to more than 1000 search engines.

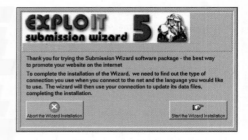

1 Download the wizard software from the Exploit site (www.exploit.net) making a note of the activation code that is displayed. The file is rather large at 6Mb, so it may take a while on a slower modem link. You may want to see if you can find the software, or a similar utility, on a magazine cover CD to save the download time.

A download point has been selected.

complete the download sequence click on the disk abo

Remember your validation code - VCexploit

Click here to change the download location

2 Once the software has installed you will get this screen which rather confusingly requires you to press the 'Start the wizard installation' button to proceed. Actually all this bit is doing is configuring the connection you use to get online.

3 And now you can start the Exploit wizard for real. The software starts by default on another confusing page, the 'update engine data files' section. You won't need to do this as it is a new installation, so click on the 'site information' tab at the left of the window.

4 That's better, a fairly straightforward form to complete that gives details of who you are, where your website is located and what it is called. You can also enter keywords and a description for your site.

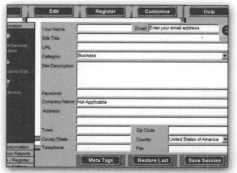

5 At the bottom of the site information screen is a button marked 'Meta Tags' which, unsurprisingly, when selected pops up this handy meta tag generator. This will automatically generate a set of keyword tags for inclusion in your web pages to try and boost your search engine status, as we explained earlier.

6 Once you have entered all the relevant information, click on the Save Session button. You will be presented with the window below which gives you the option of submitting straight away or saving the session for later. We will press the Submit Now button.

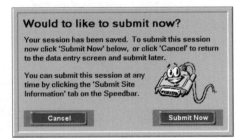

7 In the paid-for version you can select the sites you want to submit to, as many as you like for your £20 in fact. But because this is the free version the software chooses 20 sites at random for you. However, you will need to click on a search engine site anyway before selecting Start Submission.

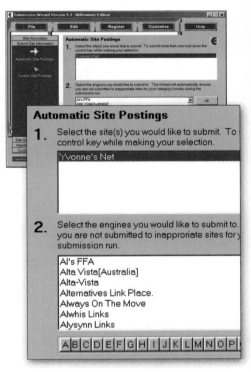

8 This status screen keeps you informed of the progress of your site submissions. It is all usually completed in a matter of minutes at the most, much faster than you could possibly fill in 20 forms yourself. When you think that the paid-for version can do the same thing for more than 1000 search sites, you may consider it £20 well spent in marketing terms.

CHAPTER 12

Publishing your site

The role of a webmaster

There is a lot more to running a website than just designing and creating the pages that go into it. A webmaster, or mistress naturally enough, has to be prepared to take on a number of tasks once the actual job of website building has been completed. These tasks may be tedious and time-consuming, such as testing that all the pages work as intended, that they display properly in the various web browsers that people might be using to, view it, and checking that all the links actually go where you expect them to, or finding the right web host to physically store your website pages and put them online, publishing your pages so that they are available for the public to look at, and updating the content regularly to keep the site fresh and keep your visitors happy.

Captain of your ship

And finally there are the more obscure and often overlooked responsibilities of a webmaster, such as ensuring that the website continues to be found in search engine listings, is marketed online to keep the traffic pouring in, and stays on the right side of the law by avoiding copyright and libel issues.

Being a webmaster, then, can be likened to being the captain of a ship but, in most cases at least, without a large crew to assist you. It is your responsibility to ensure that the engine works so that the ship sails smoothly and in the right direction, that the passengers are picked up as planned and

enjoy the facilities they were promised, and to ensure that the boat doesn't sink when the sea gets choppy.

The UK WebMasters website (www.ukwebmasters.com) offers online resources, internet-related news, reviews, and a much needed shoulder to cry on or person to turn to for advice in the many support forums.

Testing and checking

It should go without saying that you need to test and check your web pages before making them accessible to the public at large, but judging by some of the websites we encounter whilst browsing it would appear that not everyone does this. The temptation is always there, once you've finished your web page building, to quickly look at the pages using the preview function of your authoring software and then get them onto the web as soon as possible. Hold your breath, count to ten, go and make a cup of coffee, but don't press the 'publish' button just yet!

Check your code

The first thing to do is 'validate' the HTML code behind your pages. That is, to check that all the tags are entered correctly, and meet the specifications required to ensure the best fit across all the different web browser versions that are being used. To do this yourself is something of a Herculean task, not to mention a boring one. It is certainly not something that the novice web builder should consider doing, nor do they have to. There are plenty of tools available for the job. Look in the options for your web authoring software to start with; most have such a facility built in. A second opinion is always handy, so once you've uploaded your pages to the web use a utility such as Bobby (www.cast.org/bobby). This free online tool checks for the correct use of HTML, cross-browser compatibility, and also how accessible your site is for people with disabilities. Providing you correct any problems quickly, and don't publicise your site until you have done so, it's not a great problem that the pages are sitting on the web instead of your PC.

Don't forget to check the spelling of your website content; nothing can make your efforts look more amateurish than careless spelling. If your software doesn't have a spelling checker built in, use an online resource such as Doctor HTML (www2.imagiware.com/RxHTML). It will also check the structure of your page for possible problems, verify that all links are working, and will even make sure that your tables are correctly formatted for cross-browser compatibility.

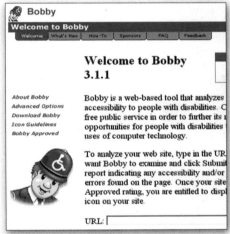

A tool like 'Bobby' (www.cast.org/bobby) will check your web pages for correct use of HTML, browser compatibility and access for people with disabilities.

Doctor HTML (www2.imagiware.com/RxHTML) will perform an online health check to ensure your web pages are fit to be seen on the web.

Testing and checking (continued)

One of the areas most often forgotten, or simply ignored, by the novice web builder is that of previewing the pages in different web browsers and at different screen resolutions. The web is a big place, and it is populated by all sorts of people using all sorts of different computers and web browser software. You cannot know what size monitor someone will be using, or how old their web browser will be. Indeed, in the US and UK browsing the web on the TV has recently become popular thanks to a service called WebTV which adds yet another dimension to the problem. Whilst the preview feature of you authoring software is useful, it isn't likely to let you see the pages in anything other than the browsers you have installed on your own computer – which means the latest versions of Internet Explorer and Netscape Navigator at best.

Different web browsers

Obviously it would be nice to have all the browsers ever made on your computer so you could test your pages in all of them, but this isn't possible for many reasons – not least that some version of the same browser cannot co-exist on the same PC. So how do you get around this issue without building a website containing nothing but plain text? Fortunately there are some excellent compromises available by way of such utilities as Browserola (www.codo.com/browserola). This emulates lots of different browser versions so you can display your pages as they would appear when seen by visitors using these older programs. It is an old tool, but a useful one. Whilst you can't guarantee that it will accurately portray your pages as seen by every browser configuration, it is better than nothing at all. Similarly, a small utility called BrowserSizer will let you preview your web pages in different screen resolutions, all at the click of a button. It works in both Internet Explorer and Netscape

Navigator and will resize the browser as seen at 640 × 480, 800 × 600, 1024 × 768 and the increasingly popular WebTV format.

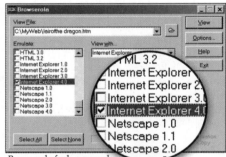

Browserola fools your web browser into thinking it is an older version of itself, or even another browser altogether.

BrowserSizer (www.applythis.com/browsersizer) simply resizes your browser window so you can see how your web pages will look to different people using different monitor sizes and screen resolutions.

Publishing your pages

You've already done the hard work and created your web pages; publishing them is the easiest bit of the whole website building business. Perhaps it is the term 'publishing' that bestows a certain mythical feel to what is, in actual fact, just the process of uploading your web files to a computer at your ISP or web hosting company.

Uploading your files

This uploading can be done using the same web authoring software that helped you build your pages, although some software handles the process better than others. The more powerful, and naturally more expensive, programs tend to do better because they have extensive management tools built in. However, this is not to say that you need to go and spend a lot of money just to publish your pages to the web. The alternative is to use one of the many programs dedicated to the task of uploading. These are known as FTP utilities, and that stands for file transfer protocol which is the technical bit behind the scenes that deals with the mechanics of moving files around the internet. There are many to choose from, but the most popular are Cute FTP and WS_FTP which are both available from any of the web's software download sites.

Don't leave anything behind

Whatever method you use, common mistakes to avoid include forgetting to upload all the files that make up your website. Most commonly people forget the image files so that no graphics appear on the published web pages. This is because the HTML files that you have uploaded only point to where the pictures should be; if you haven't uploaded them they won't be there and so can't be downloaded and displayed by visitors to your site. Perhaps the most common error is not reading the instructions given to you by your ISP or web hosting company.

These will be in the documentation sent to you when you joined up, and almost certainly will be available at their web support site. At the end of this chapter we take you step by step through the publishing process, so you can see how easy it is.

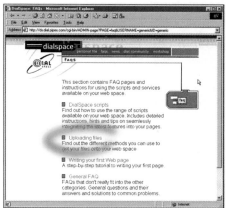

Wherever you choose to host your website, always read their instructions for publishing your pages before attempting to do upload the files. You will save a lot of time and frustration this way!

Here's Dreamweaver's built-in FTP feature. On the left are your site's 'remote' files (on the web server); to the right are your 'local' files on your PC's hard disk.

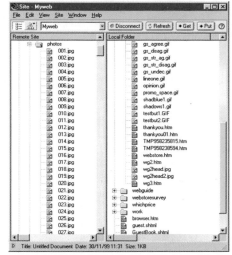

Maintaining your website

Don't think that just because your website is now published and there on the web for everyone to see that your job is over. The real truth of the matter is that now it has really only just started. If you expect your site to be a success then you have to work hard to maintain it. But what do we mean by website maintenance exactly?

Keeping current

Your web pages will undoubtedly contain links to other pages on other websites. These are known as 'external links' and can be the cause of much stress. Once every week click on each of the external links to make sure they still work; you may find that one of the pages you link to has closed down or moved to a different location, in which case you should update your page with a new link showing the correct address or remove the link altogether. You need to make sure that all the information on your site is up to date and correct; how often you do this rather depends on the type of information you publish. Some websites need updating on a daily basis, most are OK with a weekly spring clean, very few can go more than a month without starting to look dated.

Remember, an out of date, badly maintained website is worse than no website at all. In Chapter 11 we looked at ways of getting your pages noticed, which involved submitting details to search engine sites. Again, once you've given them the details and got into the listings that isn't the end of it. The conscientious

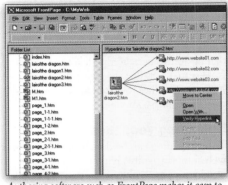

Authoring software such as FrontPage makes it easy to see exactly where the hyperlinks on your page go, and to check that they work by clicking a mouse button.

webmaster will regularly visit the main search sites and look for their own site as if they were a potential visitor. This means using search criteria that describe what your site is about, rather than its exact name or location. If it doesn't appear in the results listings you will need to refresh your submission, and possibly change those bits of your site designed for the search engines to rectify matters. Nobody said being a webmaster was easy!

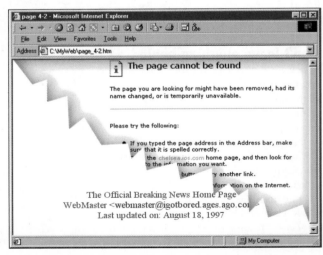

Unless your site is timeless, and most are not, it's better to have nothing at all than something that is years out of date.

Publish your first web page - step by step

Although we have established that many web authoring packages will let you publish your pages, this is not always possible. For example, the FrontPage 2000 publish wizard only works if your ISP or web host has the special FrontPage 'extensions' enabled. In any case, a program such as Cute FTP is a powerful alternative that makes the whole process as simple as using Windows Explorer to copy files from one folder to another. The only difference is that one folder is on your PC and the other is somewhere on the internet...

1 You can find the Cute FTP software on magazine cover CDs, or download it from www.cuteftp.com. Follow the installation instructions, and you will have 30 days to try it out for free before deciding if you want to buy it or not.

2 Start Cute FTP and you will see this window which looks a little confusing at first, but don't worry as all soon becomes clear. First of all you

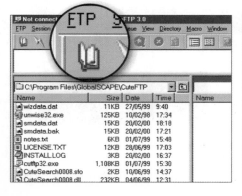

need to tell the software where your web pages are to be located. To do this click on the Site Manager button (circled).

3 The easiest thing to do is use the Connection Wizard to set things up, so click this button now. The first screen will ask you to choose an ISP, but all the companies listed are in the US – so choose 'other' and click Next. Then enter a name to call this wizard entry, 'My Web Host' is fine if you only have the one, and click Next again.

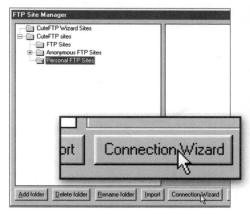

4 Now enter the FTP address that your web host or ISP has given you – this will usually start with 'ftp' or something containing ftp at least. Check with the ISP's guidelines for publishing your website if you are unsure.

87

Publish your first web page (continued)

5 Your web host or internet service provider will also have supplied you with a username and password to access your web pages; this may be the same as you use to connect to the ISP and collect your email, or it may be different. Again, check with your ISP to be sure before completing the form. (It's worth visiting your ISP's website to find general information to help with uploading your files.)

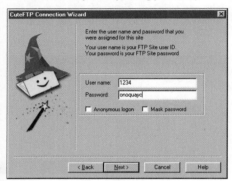

6 You can then choose a default directory on your computer, where your web pages are created, for Cute FTP to look at when it starts up instead of going to the Cute FTP installation folder. Finally, if you tick the Connect Automatically box, Cute FTP will connect to your web host FTP site each time it starts. Click on Finish to complete the configuration.

7 That is the difficult bit over and done with. Cute FTP will now connect automatically to your web host. The file explorer view on your left is your website folder on your PC, whilst on the right is your website folder on the remote web host's computer somewhere on the net. Simply drag and drop the files and folders across from your PC to the web!

8 Once all your website folders and files have been copied across, your website is published – it is as simple as that. Now you can easily change pages just by dragging and dropping updated page files across as if you were using Windows Explorer. The proof is in the pudding of course, and here is one of our example pages as seen on the web.

A

Address See URL.

Attachment A computer file or document (ie a graphic image) sent with an email.

B

Bits per second Measure of the speed a modem can handle data. 56,000 bits per second is the fastest speed possible over non-digital phone lines.

Browser Software program for navigating the internet. The two most common browsers are Netscape Navigator and Microsoft Internet Explorer.

C

Cache An area of a computer's hard disk set aside for storing web pages.

Cached files Copies of web pages you've looked at.

Channel The term used for a chatroom on IRC (see IRC).

Chatrooms A bit like the premium rate chat lines you see advertised on late night TV.

COM port Connectors through which devices such as modems plug into and communicate with your computer.

D

DHTML Dynamic HTML. An extension to HTML. Allows designers to control the appearance and position of elements on a web page.

Dialog box A window used to display a message and request input, options, or a decision from the user.

Digital signature A piece of data that can be used to verify the identity of a file's sender.

Directory services An electronic directory listing of people's email addresses and any other details they have submitted.

Used for tracking down people online.

Download To obtain a file from a website and transfer it to your PC, usually by clicking a word or icon on the web page.

Drivers Software that sits between Windows and a peripheral such as a modem, and which helps run the device for you.

E

E-commerce Selling goods and services on the internet.

Email Short for electronic mail – for sending documents between computers over the net.

F

FAQ A text file containing a list of Frequently Asked Questions. Always read FAQs before you start downloading or installing software.

Favorites/Bookmarks Your address book of links to favourite websites. Bookmark a site and you will be able to jump straight to it at a later date.

Flash memory A type of memory that retains its contents even when the PC's power is switched off.

Frames Used in web pages. One frame, say down the left hand side, may hold an index, while others may contain data such as photos. You may be able to scroll through each frame individually.

Freeware Software, often downloadable from the internet, which is then free for you to keep and use. See also Shareware.

FTP File Transfer Protocol. A method of transferring files from one computer to another across the internet. It's also

used to post HTML pages to the web.

G

Gif (Graphics Interchange Format) A type of graphics file, originally defined by the service provider Compuserve.

H

Home page This is the first page that is seen when you visit a website.

HTML editor A software program that lets you view and edit HTML code. Many editors will edit and/or create the code for you.

HTML HyperText Mark-up Language – used to create pages for the world wide web.

Hyperlink Link on a web page that takes you to another position or another web page when you click on it.

I

Internet An international network that connects millions of computers with telephone and cable links.

IP (Internet Protocol) address The unique address of a computer on the internet. It is similar to a phone number in its use.

IRC Internet Relay Chat: a system for talking to other internet users via typed messages.

ISDN A hyper-fast digital phone line. Good for downloading graphically-rich web pages quickly.

ISP Internet service provider. The companies, such as AOL, Freeserve and Demon, that provide you with access to the internet.

J

Java A special language used on websites to create ad-

Jargon buster

vanced effects, such as animated sequences and interactive buttons and menus.

K
Kbps Measurement of speed for a modem. 56Kbps is the current fastest speed available to modems.

M
Mailbox The folder in your email application that receives your incoming messages.
Mail server The computer at your ISP that handles incoming and outgoing email.
Modem A device that connects your PC to the telephone line and so to your ISP.
Moderator User who controls who can speak and about what, in a moderated chatroom.
MP3 A standard for digitally compressing music. Music files created using the standard can be downloaded quickly from the net.

N
Newsgroups Discussion areas – usually on specialised topics.

O
Offline Working with internet software without connecting your modem and phoneline.
Online If you're online, you're connected to the internet.

P
Plug and Play A computing standard devised by Intel to automate the installation and configuration of new computer hardware.
POP3 An email account that can be accessed remotely from anywhere over the internet.

Posting A message in a newsgroup.

R
RealPlayer The software required to play RealAudio and RealVideo files over the internet. Download free from www.real.com.
Registry Database used by Windows (v95 on) to store information on how your PC is configured.

S
Search engine An online service designed to take the strain out of surfing the web.
Security certificate A piece of data sent from one computer to another to prove the authenticity or security of information on the net.
Serial port An interface that can be used to plug in devices such as a modem or mouse into your PC.
Server The computer on which the actual web page files are stored.
Shareware Software that's free to download for an evaluation – if you continue to use a shareware program though you must pay for it.
Site See website.
Shockwave A program used when building many websites, which enables moving graphics. You may want to download a Shockwave viewer from www.macromedia.com to enhance your surfing.

T
Tags (HTML) Text 'tags' indicate how a browser should interpret an HTML instruction.
TCP/IP Transmission Control Protocol/Internet Protocol.

Used to transfer data and information between Computers across the internet.

U
URL Uniform Resource Locator. This is the (unique) address of a web page on the internet.
USB Universal Serial Bus A standard for connecting peripherals, such as modems and printers, to PCs.
Usenet Short for Users' Network, Usenet is a collection of public groups of messages, or newsgroup, which is accessible to a wide variety of computer systems worldwide, both on and off the internet. Writing a message that appears on Usenet is called posting.

V
V.90 The current standard for 56Kbps modems. Older 56Kbps models may be upgradable to V90.

W
Web space The amount of memory allocated to you by your ISP for you to build your own website. The more space you have the more elaborate the website can be.
Webcam Camera that links to website and displays frequently updated images.
Website Page or pages on the web, consisting of words, pictures and possibly video and sound clips, identified by the www prefix.
World wide web This is the part of the internet that most people visit using their browsers. The web is home to those colourful web pages that you will build with the help of this book.

Index

3D effect bullets 29
4AllFree 53
<A HREF= > 61
<ALT> 13
<BGSOUND> 60
<BODY> 12
<DD> 29
<DL> 29
<EMBED> 61
<FONT FACE> 30
<HEAD> 12
<HR> 13
<HTML> 12
<IMG SRC> 13
<LI> 29
<NOFRAMES> 37
<OL> 29
<TITLE> 12
<UL> 29
Abracadabra 74
Adbility 74
Adding sound 60
Adobe GoLive 22
Adobe ImageStyler 45
Adobe PageMill 22
Advertising 70
Affiliate scheme 71
ALIGN 13
Allaire HomeSite 22
AltaVista 77
Amazon 71
Amazon Associate 75
Animated banners 67
Animated GIFs 64
Animation 62
Animation Shop 67
Applets 63, 66
Arial 30
Ask Dr Web 20
Authoring software 21
Background images 28
Banner text 45
BGCOLOR 12
Bold 30
Browserola 84

BrowserSizer 84
Bullet points 29
ButtonMaker 45
CGI-scripts 49
Chat forums 52
Chatrooms 49
Checking 83
Choosing an ISP 6
Claris HomePage 22
Cnet's 'builder' pages 20
Colour 41, 43
Colour depth 44
Commission 71
Communities 22, 52, 79
Compression 41
Contact details 16
Contrast 28
CoolText 45
Copyright 18
Copyright free music 59
Copyright issues 59
Credit cards 72
Cropping images 42
Cute FTP 85
Definition list 29
Definitions 29
Descriptive text 78
Design concepts 14
Desktop Publishing 7
Digital camcorders 58
Director 65
Discussion forums 49
Do's of website design 15
Doctor HTML 83
Download times 16
Dreamweaver 22
Drop down menu 34
Drop shadows 44
eCash 72
Ecommerce 71
Effects 43
Electronic cash 72
Email 51
File sizes 40
Fireworks 45

Flash 56, 65
Formats 41
Forms 48
Frames 36
Frameset 36
Free chatroom services 52
Free clip art 24
FrontPage Express 3, 22
FrontPage extensions 49
FrontPage support 24
FTP 85
Fusion 22
GeoCities 22
GIF 41
Global market 73
Glossary 29
GoLive 22
Graphic formats 41
Graphics 40
Guest book 48, 53
Helvetica 30
Hit counter 49
Hits 70
HomeSite 22
HoTMetaL Pro 22
hotspots 44, 47
HTML 9
HTML tags 22
Hyperlinks 10, 33, 48
Hypertext 10
Image 33
Image editing software 43
Image hotspot 44
Image manipulation tools 24
Image maps 44
Images 40
ImageStyler 45
Income Café 74
Index frame 34
Indexing 37
Interactivity 10, 48
Interlaced GIFs 43
Internet Explorer 2
Internet Service Providers . . . 3
Italic 30

Index

Java 62, 66
JavaScript 66
JPEG 41
Junk email 79
Layout skills 27
Links 34
Lists 29
Logos 62
Low resolution 31
Macromedia 22
Mailing list 48
Mailto 50, 51
Maintaining your website . . . 86
Making up the page 8
Making your website pay 69
Marketing 76
Markup language 9
META tag generator 78
META tags 78, 81
Micropayments 72
Microsoft Office 25
Microsoft Word 25
MIDI files 60
Military use of the net 1
Mosaic 2
MPEG format 58
Multimedia 55
Music online 59
Namo WebEditor 22
Navigation 15, 34
Navigation bar 34, 48
NetObjects Fusion 22
Netscape Composer 3, 23
Netscape Navigator 2, 23
No cost option 23
Notepad 11, 12
Numbered lists 29
Older browsers 37
Online communities 22
Online form 49, 50
Optimising images 42
Ordered lists 29
Page properties 38
PageMill 22
Paint Shop Pro 43

Palette transparency 43
Payment Service Providers . . 72
Payments 72
Photographs 41
Pictures 40, 46
Plain text 7
Plug in Plaza 56
Plug-ins 56
PSPs 72
Publishing your site 82, 85
Quicktime 56
Radio button 50
RealPlayer 56
RealProducer 58
Resources 74
Revenue 73
Scream Design 20
Scripts 50
Search box 48
Search spiders 76
Search engines 37
Search submission wizard . . . 80
Setting up shop 71
Shadows 44
Shockwave 62, 65
SoftQuad HotMetal Pro 22
Sound 59
Spam 79
Spell checker 24, 83
Spiders 37, 77
Streaming 58
Styling 30
Submit button 50
Table cells 28
Tables 31, 32
Tag editor, tags 9, 22
Tax implications 73
Telephone lines 1
Template driven software 22
Templates 23, 24
Testing 83
Text, text editor 7, 30
Themes 24
Thumbnails 42
Tim Berners-Lee 2

Transparent background 63
Transparent GIFs 43
Tripod 22
Underlined 30
Unordered lists 29
Updating 86
Uploading your files 85
URL (Uniform
Resource Locator) 10
US government 1
Usenet newsgroups 10, 79
Validate HTML 83
Video on demand 58
Visual editor 22
Wallpaper 28
WAV 59
Web authoring software 21
Web-based animation 62
Web-based chat 52
Web browsers 2, 84
Web design software 11
Web host 49, 82
Web rings 79
WebBots 23, 24
Webcam 58
WebFX 45
Webmaster 4, 82
WebMonkey 11
WebReview 20
Website address 6
Website basics 7
Website mechanics 8
Website promotion 76
WebTV 84
What is the net? 1
Wizards 23, 25
World wide web 2
Word 2000 25
Word processors 22, 23, 25
World wide wait 40
WS_FTP 85
WYSIWYG 22, 24
Yahoo Stores 74
Yahoo! 4, 69